In the Steps of
the Great American Zoologist

William
Temple
Hornaday

*In the Steps of
the Great American Zoologist*

William
Temple
Hornaday

ꙮ

by John Ripley Forbes
Illustrations by Kathleen Elgin

ꙮ

M Evans
Lanham • New York • Boulder • Toronto • Plymouth, UK

I acknowledge with appreciation the
assistance Marjorie P. Katz gave to me in
the writing of this book.

M. Evans
An imprint of The Rowman & Littlefield Publishing Group, Inc.
4501 Forbes Boulevard, Suite 200, Lanham, Maryland 20706
http://www.rlpgtrade.com

10 Thornbury Road, Plymouth PL6 7PP, United Kingdom

Distributed by National Book Network

British Library Cataloguing in Publication Information Available

Library of Congress Cataloging-in-Publication Data Available

ISBN 13: 978-1-59077-362-8 (pbk: alk. paper)

♾™ The paper used in this publication meets the minimum requirements of
American National Standard for Information Sciences—Permanence of Paper for
Printed Library Materials, ANSI/NISO Z39.48-1992.

Printed in the United States of America

Designed by Robin Sherwood

Contents

1.	The Adventure Begins	7
2.	The Establishment	22
3.	Setting Out	31
4.	A Year in the Jungle	45
5.	Stuffed Animals	56
6.	The Near Extermination of the American Bison	66
7.	Zoo Building	80
8.	Forty Years' War for Wild Life	92
	Nature Projects You Can Do	109
	Bibliography	128

1
The Adventure Begins

Two rifle shots rang out along the shore. An enormous crocodile, wounded, angry, and deadly dangerous, made its way across a sandbar to the edge of the Orinoco River. Not far away, two hunters stood watching the beast they had been attempting to kill. The hunters were Chester Jackson and William Temple Hornaday.

The injured animal was halfway across the sandbar when young Hornaday suddenly dropped his weapon and began to run after it. He hoped to head it off before it vanished into the water.

"You fool, Bill! Don't go near him!" Chet shouted, frantically working an empty shell out of his rifle where it had stuck fast.

Ignoring his friend's warning, Hornaday caught up with the fleeing crocodile. "Bring my rifle, quick!" he called, trying to get behind the animal to grab its tail. Just then, it turned swiftly around and lifted its head high above the sand. Its jaws gaped open, its double row of terrifying teeth only a foot away from the young hunter.

Chet answered angrily. "You young fool! Get away from there!" By then his rifle was ready for action. One more bullet went crashing into the neck of the crocodile. And in a matter of minutes the once-dangerous beast was dead.

"What in the name of heaven were you thinking about anyway?" Chet asked, still angry. "You could have held a train of cars as easily as him. I thought he was going to grab you up and run into the water with you!"

"I just wanted to keep him busy and keep his mind off the water while you came up and finished him," Hornaday replied in a shaky voice. "Come on, let's get that tough hide off him, just to change the subject."

Soon the two men were absorbed in the painstaking task of skinning the crocodile.

Twenty years old, Bill Hornaday had come to the jungles of Venezuela to kill wild animals. His mission was to bring their skins and skeletons back to Rochester, New York, where he was employed at Ward's Natural Science Establishment. There they would be mounted for display and sold to museums all over the country. If his expedition was successful and he returned to Rochester with a good supply of jungle beasts, perhaps Professor Ward would finally consent to the East Indies trip that he had been trying to wangle. Even as a boy on his father's farm, he had

8

dreamed of those distant dark green jungles. As much as he was enjoying his present adventure, he could not help wishing he had been able to talk Professor Ward into that other trip instead.

He realized, of course, that he had come just about as close to his boyhood dreams as any twenty-year-old might hope. How many others of his age born in Plainfield, Indiana, had managed to have such adventures in South America? None at all, he guessed.

William was born in December, 1854, six years before the Civil War. He was the youngest of several sons. His father was a farmer. When he was almost four the family and its flocks and horses outgrew their lovely little farm. Although they knew they would miss the clear streams and blue grass of central Indiana, and their relatives in and about nearby Indianapolis, they decided to move to Iowa to a larger farmstead. They had relatives there, too.

William and his mother and the household belongings were settled in covered wagons. The men—his father, his older brothers, and several hired hands—drove the horses and guided the flocks and herds that followed along behind. It was a typical pioneer wagon train, a familiar sight in those days.

One sunny afternoon their journey took them alongside a branch line of the Chicago and Indianapolis Railroad. Railroad trains, and the wood-burning, smoke-belching locomotives that pulled them, were a much less familiar sight than wagon trains. The little boy had never seen one. Neither had most of the horses.

When they came to a curve in the railroad tracks,

they looked north and saw a locomotive with a passenger train rushing, it seemed, right toward them.

"Hold those horses!" shouted his father, realizing that they were about to bolt in panic. "Everyone out! Grab the bridles! Quick! Get out, everybody!"

Instantly the wagons halted, and everyone obeyed. William, the littlest pioneer, was right near the railroad fence, next to the lead team of horses. He could hear the awful roar of the locomotive. He was terrified. Nothing in his brief experience of the world had prepared him for this. He looked up and saw a big black monster racing directly at him.

Before his mother knew what was happening, he dashed toward what seemed to him to be a safe place —underneath one of the horses. He didn't know— how could he?—that the horses were as frightened as he, and might run at any second. If they did, he would be crushed under the wagon.

He heard his mother scream. "William! Someone save William!"

One of the farm workers reached under the wagon and snatched the boy to safety. Another held the horses, which even then were stamping, trying to run.

But he learned that the locomotive was not to be feared, that it made a great noise but stayed on its own path. The wagon train reorganized itself and the pioneer trek continued.

The farm in Eddyville, three miles south of the Des Moines River, was a wonderful place for a boy to grow up. He had chores to do, of course; and he got some schooling. But mostly he could watch the changing seasons, the wild roses when they came, and the virgin Iowa prairie. He chased the prairie chickens, quail, ground squirrels, pocket gophers, and hundreds of kinds of prairie birds. When the family went back to visit their relatives living along Eagle Creek in Indiana there were different animals to become acquainted with—turtles, yellow perch, little green herons.

It was on the Iowa farm that he had his "first interview with a skunk." As he told it afterward, "the meadow larks were sweetly warbling, and all Nature was smiling and glad, when a big, bad skunk suddenly rose out of the landscape. He was a perfect whale of a skunk. He was heavily armed, and I was not. He carried a deadly revolver. He faced me. His beady, black eyes glared. He made a series of short runs at me,—snarling, showing his teeth, and stamping on the ground with his black front feet, most defiantly. Few and short were the words we said."

As William imagined it, the skunk said: "Run, you little skeezicks! Run, or it will be the worse for you."

"You get off this prairie," the boy answered. "You are too fresh."

"I dare you to try to put me off," the skunk said. "If you dast to try it, I'll make you bury your clothes for four weeks."

Realizing that the skunk meant business, the boy whistled three times. It was a signal. William's older brother Calvin, working on another part of the farm, came running with his new shotgun in his hand. And that was the end of that skunk.

A sudden encounter with six big and beautiful white birds on the same bit of prairie provided a dif-

12

ferent experience, however. The sight of them shining in the sun was so thrilling to the boy that he could not sleep. His impression of those birds would stay with him always. And years later, at college, his vivid recollection would be matched by an illustration in a book, and he would be able to identify them as whooping cranes.

William's father and brothers were all crack rifle shots, and Calvin undertook to teach the boy how to shoot. The first lesson involved a gray squirrel which, together, they spotted in the top branches of a large maple tree. William was given a Kentucky rifle, put in position, and told how to use it. Then Calvin crept around to the other side of the tree to distract the squirrel.

It worked. The younger boy easily shot the small animal, and it fell to the ground.

As he picked it up he felt the thrill of catching his first game, but only for an instant. Then it seemed to him that it had been too easy. The squirrel was just posing there for him. He had gotten it on his first shot. "The squirrel didn't have a chance!" he said sadly. "It's unfair, and it's no fun at all."

But he did learn how to shoot. He became quite good at it. He used this skill sparingly, however, while he was growing up. Over a period of time he shot a blue jay, a green heron, two prairie chickens, and a woodpecker. He examined their plumage; he looked at them thoroughly, to see how they were made and put together and what they were fitted to do. The chickens at least could be eaten. But the heron, the jay, and the woodpecker had to be thrown away. He was disappointed, and somehow he felt guilty for having taken life, even a bird's life, to no purpose.

When he reached sixteen he thought it time to consider his future seriously. He knew farm life. He loved animals. He had learned to tend and doctor them. He could handle a gun as well as anyone he knew. But he definitely did not wish to become a farmer.

His parents had both died a few years earlier, and his uncle, with whom he had gone to live, was his guardian. It was his uncle's idea that the teenager learn dentistry, but William decided that he would like to become a newspaper editor. He realized after thinking about it, however, that, although he could claim to be "a corking good speller and could write some," he didn't have sufficient education to become a country editor. He knew that he must go to college.

But how, when and where? These were the big questions.

He had heard of the Iowa State College at Ames. And so he sent for the catalogue and studied it thoroughly. His schooling in Knoxville met the entrance requirements: that would be no problem. But there was no money available to pay for his tuition or living expenses. he would have to try for a scholarship.

Only two students from each county in the state could hold scholarships at a time, however, and Marion County was already over its quota with six. It would be years, he realized, before he could enroll from his home county. Then he had an inspiration. About twenty miles away was Oskaloosa College, in Mahaska County. He could probably scrape up enough money to enroll there for a year of preparatory study while living at home. Then, under the Mahaska County scholarship quota, which was usually unfilled, he could apply to Ames.

Everything went according to schedule: after a year at Oskaloosa William went to Ames. He took courses in zoology, botany, stock-breeding, forestry, surveying, map-making, and free-hand drawing. He was letting his interests and inclinations lead him. At the same time he was laying a sound cornerstone for the career he would build in later years.

The State College at Ames was starting a museum. A friendly sophomore told William, who was a freshman, that a ten-dollar reward had been offered by the college president the year before to anyone who could mount a specimen and thereby prove himself capable of caring for the growing collection.

William had once seen the zoology professor at Oskaloosa prepare and mount a crow, and so he thought he knew how.

With great self-confidence he went looking for a small animal in the nearby woods. He found a dead gray squirrel and brought it back. With broomwire, hemp fiber known as tow, shoe buttons for eyes, and a hickory nut as a prop, he went to work, skinning, cleaning, stuffing, and mounting the squirrel. He got the squirrel to sit up, and proudly went to show his work to President Welch.

"Not good enough," was the verdict, delivered without any encouragement whatever.

This encounter left William full of dismay. Fortunately, a young man who was a teacher of zoology and botany, Professor Charles E. Bessey, became aware of William's aspirations and took an interest in him. One day near the end of the school year Professor Bessey invited William to come to his office.

"Now, young man, we're going to see how much you know about taxidermy! I've got a fresh bird for you, and if you mount it decently you may yet get to work in our museum."

"Show me the victim," said the freshman, outwardly brave but inwardly nervous about the unexpected test.

Professor Bessey lifted up some newspapers that were spread out over what had appeared to be a lump in the carpet. An enormous snow-white pelican was uncovered, its body like a great pillow of down, its bill looking as long as a fence rail to the would-be taxidermist. It had been shot down while flying north, its seasonal migration having taken it right over the campus.

Next, Professor Bessey showed young Hornaday a large book, handsomely bound in morocco leather. It was John James Audubon's famous *Birds of North America*. "There," he exclaimed, as he opened it and placed it on his desk. "This is a fine picture of your bird, the Great White Pelican. You can shape and pose him from it."

The Audubon book stunned the student. When, years later, he stopped to think about it, he wrote of it as the discovery of a New World. It told him not only how to mount his pelican, but more important, that there was such a thing as a professional naturalist; that one could make a career out of working with

17

animals and still be neither a college teacher nor a farmer. It told him that, far from Iowa, there were zoological museums that contained many stuffed and mounted specimens, where men could become absorbed in learning the hows and whys of nature. And it identified for him the wonderful Whooping Crane of his boyhood.

"Now, young man," Professor Bessey challenged him, interrupting his thoughts. "Can you mount that bird?"

"Yes, Sir!" the boy answered. "But you must help me get some tools and materials together."

All went well while he skinned, cleaned, and stuffed the bird, and posed it following Audubon's painting. But when it came time to fasten the stiff wires that held the bird in position, the old pliers he had been given to work with nearly failed him. After a struggle, however, his determination carried the day. And with justifiable pride he was able to display the bird.

His reward soon followed. He was given the post of taxidermist and custodian of the school museum.

The museum, such as it was, was now his, to do with whatever he would, and could. It contained about two hundred birds, perched, with the aid of some loose wires, on wooden pegs, an assortment of unmounted game birds, cranes, and ducks, and a row of empty cabinets with shelves and glass doors. The remainder of the semester and most of the following school year were spent in getting as many of these as possible into shape, and setting them up in the cabinets. Helping the student taxidermist was one small book, an old English *Manual of Taxidermy*. But when

it came to teaching him how to arrange the neck feathers of a heron so the bird would look decent enough to be put on public view, or how to remove grease and caked blood from delicate plumage so that the true colors, and not an unsightly stain, would greet the eye, the volume was of no use. Frustrated, William vowed not only to learn the art of taxidermy to perfection but, when he should master it, to write his own manual. He would write it so plainly and illustrate it so clearly "that any farm boy could learn from its pages how to clean and preserve and mount birds and animals." He had as yet only an inkling of how much he himself still had to learn. Twenty years later he would keep the vow he made as a student at Ames.

During his second year he came to a definite decision about his future. One afternoon he was walking alone across the campus. He paused in a great open space and then made his resolution. "I will be a zoologist. I will be a museum-builder. I will fit myself to be a curator. I will learn taxidermy under the best living teachers—and I will become one of the best in that line. That will make a steppingstone for travel. for field studies of animals, and for work in a museum. This settles it! I will bring wild animals to the millions of people who cannot go to them!"

Having no idea of how to go about achieving his goal, he confided in Professor Bessey. And a few days later, while William was at work in his museum, Bessey dashed into the room, a copy of the latest issue of the *American Naturalist* magazine in his hand.

20

"See here, Hornaday! Listen to this! Keep working while I read it to you."

He had come upon an article describing Ward's Natural Science Establishment in Rochester, New York, where there was a workshop in which zoologists, taxidermists, osteologists, and other technicians prepared fresh animal specimens for museum display. Ward, a professor at the University of Rochester, hired experienced workers trained in the museums of Europe, as well as a select group of promising young American men.

Professor Bessey and William lost no time in deciding that a job with Henry Ward was the next step. And that very night a letter went from Ames to Rochester. William asked to be accepted and given the opportunity "to learn taxidermy in all its branches, and salary no object."

A prompt reply from Ward brought encouragement, but not final acceptance. Then both Professor Bessey and President Welch wrote to Rochester recommending their prize student, and in due time he was accepted.

In November of 1873, at the age of nineteen, William Temple Hornaday left the state where he had spent most of his life until that time. He was off to Ward's, where he expected to "spend at least two years in intensive museology work and study." His salary was to be six dollars a week.

2
The Establishment

Professor Ward had been, twenty years earlier, very much like Hornaday himself. The professor came from a rural part of New York not far from where his business, known as the Establishment, would later be located. He too had been an impoverished student deeply interested in the natural sciences. His opportunity came when a well-to-do school friend took him along as his companion on a three-year European trip that included a period of study at the School of Mines in Paris, and a period of adventure up the Nile and through the Egyptian desert.

In Paris, Ward started to make a collection of rocks and minerals found on field trips and to sell duplicates to students, professors, and museums. He soon began to do the same thing with fossils and skeletons. In the course of his travels he came to Bonn, in Germany. There a Dr. Kranz had a place of business called the Establishment where geological and zo-ological specimens were prepared and sold to museums and colleges all over Europe. And it was then that Ward was inspired to create a similar institution back in Rochester.

Continuing his travels, he sent trunkloads of specimens back home to await the day when he would open a place of his own. When he did, in 1860, his stock-in-trade consisted of forty thousand specimens: semi-precious stones, great blocks of basalt, glass models of the Kohinoor and other famous diamonds, plaster casts of fossilized shellfish, reptiles, and mammals.

By the time William arrived, Ward's Establishment consisted of a cluster of buildings located near the University of Rochester, where Ward spent some of his time teaching botany and zoology. William's first tasks consisted of piling up empty boxes, scraping and cleaning plaster casts of fossils, and digging drains. He was also "Head Pumper," as he called it, in the "water-logged cellar of Professor Ward's new and handsome house." This went on for three months, and although the newcomer was happy just to be there surrounded by skeletons and animal skins, he had yet to get his hands on any of them. Then he decided it was time to remind someone of his original interest in learning taxidermy.

He was transferred to the Taxidermy Building, where he was taken into the skin room. It smelled strongly of camphor and creosote, used to preserve the skins until they could be worked on. The skins of animals from every corner of the world were here.

The foreman of the department told the young man to choose one, but he was so bewildered by the wealth of opportunity before his eyes that he let the foreman make the selection for him. "It was," he always remembered, "a humble seal."

Working here, he watched the experienced taxidermists closely. Although he knew that he had a great deal to learn, he recognized that there was something wrong with the way the animals were being shaped. No wild monkey ever had round, stick-like legs. And the torso of a deer looked clumsy after being tightly packed with straw. He was quite sure of this, although neither monkeys nor deer frequented the prairie where he had lived. But the young man took it all in, secretly rebelling, but remaining quiet about it for the time being. After all, the Establishment was the home of what was then the best taxidermy in America. So he continued to work, with specimens by day, studying from every available book by night. He was absorbing the zoology of the world.

After three months of taxidermy, William was ready for adventure. His boyhood dreams had been revived by the exotic specimens that arrived at Ward's daily. Impatient, he felt that his chance for travel and adventure was now or never. He must go on a field trip as a zoological collector for the Establishment. But his hints to Professor Ward went unheeded. And so he decided to force the issue.

One evening in May he casually visited Ward's private study and quietly announced, "I am going to West Africa for gorillas. Can I do anything in particular for you while I'm there?" His tone sounded quite

as though he were offering to go on an errand to the general store across the street. But it had the desired effect of startling Ward into action. Wheeling around in his swivel chair, he asked for details.

"I have eight hundred dollars right now, and I can put my hands on another thousand in a few weeks," William explained. "I'm ready for field work, and I intend to make an investment only in a trip that's worth while."

Struck by this businesslike approach, Ward began to take the matter seriously. The two settled down to talk. Ward decided that he would put up half of the money required for expenses, and share in the returns. They started outlining the details—what to hunt for and where, the equipment that would be needed, people Ward knew who might be helpful.

William lost little time in informing his Iowa relatives of his expedition. He was so excited he could think of little else.

An uncle soon appeared in Rochester.

"Now then, let's talk this matter over," he said. He offered William a business position in Buffalo, paying seventy-five dollars a month. But young Hornaday would not be tempted.

"Now Billy, you're only nineteen, and that's far too young to go to Africa afoot and alone. I don't want you to leave your bones somewhere in the jungle. And I'll give you five hundred dollars as a gift if you'll just abandon that plan."

It was nice to be so highly regarded by one's relatives. "Well, Uncle," William said, "I can't disregard your feelings and judgment. But I can't rob you of your five hundred dollars either." He thought for a minute. "All right. I'm willing to make my first expedition to some less dangerous place, one that you can approve."

The uncle was satisfied, but made sure to enlist the cooperation of Professor Ward before leaving. Ward, impressed by the concern of the family, promised to break William in more gradually. And so a trip to Cuba and Florida was planned instead.

Several weeks of hunting in Cuba netted William only some parrots, some small crocodiles, a few Cuban tree rats, and several large birds. Disappointed, he sailed from there across Florida Strait to Key West, where he collected "a fine lot of big tropical fishes, huge loggerhead and green turtles, corals, shells, sponges and various other spoils of the sea." That was more like it.

William's next stop was Miami, then an untouched jungle. He traveled there on a small boat. On board he fell into conversation with a young farmer from Wisconsin who had come to Florida for adventure. After two hours they decided to join forces in exploring Biscayne Bay and the Everglades. The farmer was Chester Jackson.

Miami in 1874 consisted of three houses. Living in them were two families and a half dozen laborers who had come to build the city. The day after Jackson and Hornaday arrived the workers captured a big diamondback rattlesnake which the hunters received for their collection. This was an auspicious start. But the week that followed did not come up to their expectations.

Hiring a small boat, they went up the bay, looking for the hiding places of animals. At Arch Creek, where a large mass of stone formed a natural bridge over the waterway, they were told of an old alligator that was frequently seen in the area. The creature was reported to be extremely large, and quite clever, having escaped capture many times.

Early next morning they were in their boat and heading down the creek. They had gone about a mile when, on the bank, they saw the reptile. Through his telescope Hornaday could see that he was gray and had a sharp snout, with a long tooth protruding from it. He did not look at all like the flat-nosed, black Florida alligators. An alligator's long teeth were hidden when its mouth was closed. Could this be a crocodile? In Florida? Impossible! Everyone knew that there were no crocodiles in Florida, or any place else in the United States for that matter. Of course, he had only a month ago captured some in Cuba. But they were very small, and this beast was enormous. He kept watching it, puzzling over its appearance. And while he was still observing it, the animal vanished into the water. That put an end to the day's hunt.

Next morning they set out again, camouflaging their boat with branches of jungle trees. The reptile again seemed to have sensed their presence, for he again disappeared under water.

The third day, impatient and more curious than ever, they started out even earlier, hoping to catch the animal while it still slept. The plan worked. They rowed silently to a tangled clump of mangrove roots at the shore, and there Hornaday got out of the boat and hid in ambush. Jackson rowed just around the bend in the creek, from which point he could quickly return at the first crack of a rifle.

After a wait of half an hour Hornaday saw the beast come to the surface in the middle of the stream and look around. There was now no doubt about the nature of the quarry. It was definitely a crocodile that he would shoot today!

For a nerve-wracking quarter of an hour he waited, watching as it floated around in the water, expecting it to come out on the bank for its daily sunbath at any moment. But the crocodile would not leave the safety of the water. Finally, even though he knew that the animal, if wounded, would go under, he obeyed the impulse to shoot, hoping to grab it in time. He aimed for the right eye, and sent a .40-caliber bullet directly into it. The bullet destroyed the eye and chipped a piece of bone out of the skull above it.

He would never forget what happened next. He would often tell the story of how "that big reptile went plumb crazy," first thrashing the water, then diving to the bottom, and then sending four feet of an enormous tail shooting straight up out of the water. Jackson, who had started rowing as if his life depended on it the instant he heard Hornaday fire, came around the bend. Quickly he aimed his rifle, but it was an old, unreliable weapon, and missed fire. Not taking time to adjust it, Chet kept rowing. In the boat was his fishing spear. Meeting the thrashing beast head on in the middle of the creek, he stood up in the boat, aimed at the head of the animal and gave a vicious thrust with his spear.

The crocodile was pierced. But that strong creature rolled over and snapped the tip right off the spear! He was wounded, but still free.

Chet rowed hastily to the mangrove clump and Hornaday clambered into the boat. They followed the crocodile as it careened through the water, Hornaday firing bullet after bullet into the back of its neck, hoping one of his shots would land in the neck vertebrae or brain of his moving target. At last the weary beast allowed himself to be cornered in a shallow inlet, and there he died.

Next, they had to get him up to the Arch. They tied him to their boat, but it seemed to Hornaday that they "might as well have tried to tow a steamroller" as to pull that fourteen-foot-long monster with their small craft. Nevertheless, they managed to do it. Hornaday skinned the crocodile perfectly, and, later that year, proudly saw it sold to the U.S. National Museum for $250. It was displayed at the Centennial Exposition in Philadelphia. Hornaday wrote an article about *Crocodilus floridanus* for the *American Naturalist,* and created a sensation in the zoological world with his discovery.

Before leaving Florida he and Jackson had found its mate, too. And as the climax to what was, all in all, an extremely successful first field expedition for Bill Hornaday, Professor Ward, who was quite impressed, said he would be happy to send his protégé, the very next month, to the West Indies and South America. Chester Jackson, having proved his competence and having nothing better to do, went along also.

3
Setting Out

Hornaday's "bag" from the Venezuelan expedition included deer, otter, two species of macaw, armored and cannibal fish, terrapins, howler monkeys, water hogs, a jaguar, an anaconda, an electric eel, a puma, and several guacharao birds as well as their nests and eggs.

He was rewarded for his adventures when he got back to Rochester. Even Professor Ward was impressed with the collection of skins and skeletons. Soon he was planning to send his young apprentice on a three-year expedition. Until that time most of his specimens had been purchased from hunters abroad. But this was not always satisfactory. Ward had been completely unable to obtain skins or skeletons of the Indian crocodile, despite the large sums he had offered to hunters in the East Indies. He figured that if Hornaday spent six weeks looking for members of the species *Gavialis gangeticus* in their native habitat near the Ganges River, he could bring back about twenty-five specimens. That alone would make a journey to India worth while.

Professor Ward decided to take a working vacation for a few months and to join Hornaday on the first part of the trip. Together they set out in October, 1876. They would travel through Europe and down to Egypt. After that, Hornaday had a "roving commission to visit India, Ceylon, the Malay Peninsula, and Borneo, in quest of mammals in particular, and vertebrates of all kinds in general." He particularly reveled in the fact that "quadrupeds of all species, from the elephant downward, were needed most of all," and that his "natural preference for the chase and study of mammals in their haunts was to be indulged almost without limit."

They worked their way down through Europe, visiting museums, schools, and private collections. Belfast, Edinburgh, Sheffield (where Hornaday stopped to have two dozen skinning knives, of the best steel, made from his own pattern), and London. Here he spent days in the British Museum, studying specimens of the fauna he hoped to bring back in the coming months.

Paris, Turin, Milan, Florence, Pisa, Rome. The two of them spent hours together in the natural history museums. "And surreptitiously," Hornaday wrote in the journal he had resolved to keep, "I did the art museums alone." He thought of Rome as "a desert for natural history," a city that did not "care a whit for nature unless it is reproduced in paint or marble."

Naples, where they "spent eight delightful days in spite of beggars and bad smells," was more to their taste. Two trips to Vesuvius netted a ton of lava to ship back to Rochester. At Pompeii they "scooped up a bagful" of the fine ash that still covered the city, eighteen hundred years after it was buried by the nearby volcano.

In Naples also they spent days along the quays lining the bay shore, buying shells and shellfish from the fishermen, which they preserved in spirits. It seemed to Hornaday that "the Italians eat every living animal they can catch in the sea excepting the corals and sponges." He and Ward experimented with some local delicacies purchased at the oyster-stalls. The stewed octopus was "as tough as india-rubber and salt as the ocean." But, somewhat to their surprise, "very good" was the verdict after they tasted fried shark.

Next stop was Egypt. They steamed into the port of Alexandria five days after leaving Naples, and found it even dirtier and smellier than the city they had just left. They were glad to start the railroad trip of one hundred and thirty-one miles across Egypt to Cairo. Flat and fertile delta land was succeeded by ruined villages, bits of desert, and the sight of the Pyramids. Finally they approached Cairo in a cloud of sand and dust.

They went at once to the best place in town, the Grand New Hotel, and set to work to collect and prepare their animal specimens. "But it wouldn't do, and we might have known it before going there," Hornaday wrote in his diary. "The high-toned guests of the hotel wondered too much and looked too much scandalized when we began to buy ibex skulls, stuffed mastigures (scaly lizards), polypterus (an African fish), and other queer animals, and carry them upstairs to our rooms."

It did not take these travelers long to discover that "a naturalist who intends to accomplish anything has no business to stop at a grand hotel." So they transferred to the smaller Hotel de l'Europe, and were soon located in ground-floor rooms. Here natives bearing odd animals to sell came to bargain with them, and here they happily prepared and packed their specimens, and sawed and hammered at the packing boxes.

A trip to a petrified forest was the occasion for Hornaday's first camel ride. It was strenuous exercise, for at every step the camel heaved him forward and then stopped suddenly. He was doubled over every other minute. But he enjoyed it nonetheless. At the forest they gathered the petrified wood and also some fossil oyster shells. At noon they spread a tablecloth over the clean brown sand of a small hill, and feasted on claret, oranges, dates, and sandwiches. The trip back to Cairo was better. The fossils rode the camel, and Hornaday had a donkey.

Finally the end of their Egyptian visit approached. Professor Ward planned to spend some time at the port of Jidda, near Mecca, on the Red Sea, and gather invertebrates and fish there. Hornaday was scheduled to leave his employer and continue on to India.

Accordingly, he boarded the *Memfi*. The other passengers, except for a British officer who, with his wife and child, was returning to his post near the Khyber Pass, were all Moslem pilgrims returning from Mecca to Bombay.

The officer was Colonel Ross, a virtual encyclopedia of practical information. He taught the hunter a few useful phrases of Hindi, including "Are there any large crocodiles near here?"

Mrs. Ross was good company, too. Hornaday credited her with diagnosing a "malady" which had been bothering him lately. It was named "the blues" and, she told him, it came from "envy and selfishness." Her prescription, which he found effective, was: "Go to work vigorously to promote the happiness of those around you, and thereby forget yourself."

Actually, he was homesick, although he never used the word. He was heading for the strangest part of the world, where not a place or a person was known to him. He had taken leave of Professor Ward, his last link with home, and he was lonely. He missed his family in Iowa—it was now three years since he had been there—but most of all he missed a certain young lady, Miss Josephine Chamberlain of Battle Creek, Michigan. They had become engaged in between the time he had returned from South America and the time he set out with Professor Ward.

Fighting his temporary unhappiness, Hornaday resolved to follow Mrs. Ross's advice. And he carefully kept all references to the "Empress Josephine," as he called his lady, out of his journal. He set his mind firmly on the business before him.

Just before midnight on January 16, 1877, they

came in sight of Bombay, and in the early morning hours the *Memfi* anchored in the harbor. As soon as possible he was rowed ashore in a small boat. He had to look for a place to stay.

He had learned his lesson in Cairo. Now, just around the corner from Watson's, the best hotel in town, he came upon Doughty's Hotel. He thought, "It's a little nest of a place, and would hardly make a kitchen for Watson's. But for my purposes it's ideal."

He moved in and hired his first Indian servant. Carlo could speak about fifty words of English, and was destined to be his helper and companion for several months.

He was fascinated by the life of the streets—people dressed in strange garments, animals pulling carts or just wandering in and out. Many carts were being pulled by buffaloes, the Indian beasts of burden. "It surely is the homeliest quadruped that ever breathed," he thought. "It's just a huge skeleton covered with a nearly hairless blue-black rubbery skin." But it so interested him that he went before sunrise the next morning to the market where the butcher trains came in. He purchased five large buffalo heads and brought them back to Doughty's. After breakfast he and Carlo set to work in the hotel courtyard to clean them.

His main interest was the fish market, where he bought sharks, shark-rays, and skates. He was most excited about some large rays. He prepared the skeleton of one and the skin of another.

But after a week in Bombay he felt he had exhausted the possibilities the city offered for collecting. He

decided to leave for Allahabad, a place where the Ganges and Jumna rivers meet. He was after crocodiles, and both rivers were said to be filled with them.

He said goodbye to the Ross family, and Captain Ross gave him letters of introduction to two of his brothers. One of them, a lawyer, lived in Allahabad. He shipped a large case of prepared specimens ahead to Calcutta, and he and Carlo set out.

When he got to Allahabad, he lost no time in calling on lawyer Ross with his letter of introduction. He was in luck, for the third brother, a major in the British Army, was there for a few days. They both "received me with the utmost cordiality," he wrote, "and the three of us sat down directly to a council of war in reference to my movements." The topic under discussion was the best place to find the large Indian crocodile, *Gavialis gangeticus*, or gavial.

The two Rosses agreed that the Jumna had more and bigger crocodiles than the Ganges. If Hornaday should be unsuccessful here, he was invited to continue on up the Jumna to Etawah, 206 miles away, where Major Ross was stationed. The major assured the young hunter that large crocodiles were to be found in that vicinity, and other tempting animals as well.

With the assistance of Carlo he hired a boat with a roomy deck and three boatmen, put a supply of food on board, and spent five days going up and down the Jumna searching for gavials. He collected several large birds—vultures and sea eagles among them. He shot an otter but he could find only two very small gavials. And so he set out for Etawah.

On his very first afternoon there, walking along the river, he saw three large crocodiles on a sandbar, but they were too far from shore for him to shoot. A little later a friend of Major Ross's, hunting with him, shot a five-foot one at a more accessible spot. This man had also bagged a saras crane earlier in the afternoon, and so there were two valuable specimens, and promise of more to come, to show for the first day.

"A good omen," Hornaday thought, paying some native boys to bring the crane and the croc back to where he was staying.

The next morning he was hard at work skinning both of them, and eager to take full advantage of what he recognized as good hunting ground.

He hired a large flat-bottomed boat, had an awning of grass thatch built over a portion of the deck as a shield from the midday sun, and laid in a three weeks' supply of staples—rice, flour, bread, sugar, onions, butter. This would be enough for himself, Carlo, and the five natives he had hired to operate the boat and help him. Meat and fish they would provide as they went along.

Floating down the muddy, crooked river, borne alone by its swift current, he realized that it would not be easy to bag his crocodiles. He had long ago learned that it was best to shoot these animals on dry land, for if killed while in the water they would sink. He had to get them while they rested on the river bank or a sandbar. Furthermore, his first shot had to be a good one, for if the animal were merely wounded it would soon be up and away. He had to at least stun the animal so that one of his men could get to it and grab its tail to keep it from going into the stream. If he shot at the brain he would only succeed in blowing off the top of the head, and then neither the skin nor the skeleton would be fit for use. And even if he shot at the heart or lungs the beast could still get away. He must aim for the neck or shoulders, in order to strike the vertebral column and break the spinal cord. Then the crocodile's jaws would spring wide open, the legs would draw up convulsively, and the animal would be instantly stilled, waiting for the final blow to fall.

He spent the first afternoon practicing his distance shooting, for he knew he would have to be a better shot than ever before. Early the next morning he shot his first gavial, a ten-footer, but it got away. The first two shots did not paralyze it, and it was able to get into the water. A third shot did the trick, but his men, on their first try, hesitated to grab the scaly long tail, and it slithered into the Jumna just beyond their reach. He was disgusted with himself for his poor shooting, and with his men for their timidity. He resolved he would do better next time. And he gave his men a lecture. "I shamed them for their cowardice," he wrote in his diary, "and pointed out how the reptile was too nearly dead to bite anyone. I told them that if any one of them should ever be bitten by a gavial I would send him to the hospital and pay him double wages until he should get well, and that if any one should be drowned while trying to catch one for me, I would give his widow a hundred rupees. This harangue had a wonderful effect upon them."

The next day they all worked better. An eleven-

footer was stopped with the very first shot, and three of the boatmen swam to the sandbar and grabbed it by the tail. A mile further down the river a slightly smaller one was taken. Then they stopped to dissect the two reptiles.

They moored the boat at the river bank, and pulled the crocodiles out onto the sand. Hornaday and Carlo rolled up their sleeves, sharpened their knives, and prepared to work, while the boatmen watched them. Dozens of vultures, crows, and hawks gathered to watch them, too, and so did dozens of native men and boys.

Hornaday had decided to prepare the skeleton of the larger crocodile. First he measured the animal and made a careful note of its dimensions. Slitting the skin open along the underside from the throat to the tip of the tail, he cut it away from the body. Then he cut the front legs at the shoulders and the hind legs at the hips to separate them from the torso. Carefully he and Carlo removed the flesh from the bones of each leg and foot. Occasionally they would throw large pieces of crocodile meat to the scavenger birds that had gathered to watch the proceedings, and they were amused by the greedy shrieking as the birds fought over the scraps.

Then the head and tail were cut off, and the animal lay before them in seven parts. They removed the flesh from the head, torso, and tail, piece by piece, until only the bones were left. Then they took the vital organs out of the torso.

After the flesh had been removed from the entire skeleton, all the bones and the ligaments that connected them were brushed thoroughly with strong arsenical soap, in order to keep the ligaments from decaying and to protect the bones from rats and insects. Hornaday himself had made this preparation before leaving Rochester. It was a mixture of melted white soap with arsenic, camphor, and potash stirred in. He had taken along thirty pounds of it, packed in earthenware jars. When he wanted to use it he would dissolve some of it in water until he had a thick liquid, and then he would paint it on the bones with a paint brush.

Now he could pack the skull, tail, and the four legs inside the cavity of the torso, and tie the bundle with strong twine. In a few days the skeleton would be perfectly dry and hard. It would never develop a bad odor. He could pack it compactly in a box.

It would have taken him, experienced as he now was, five hours to prepare one such skeleton single-handed. Fortunately he had trained Carlo to assist him, and so he had time to work on the second crocodile before evening. He planned to preserve the skin of this beast.

He measured the second animal with special care, for when it came time to stuff it these measurements would be the guide by which a life-like crocodile would be shaped. Next he divided the skin along the middle of the belly, from the throat to the tip of the tail, making one long straight cut. Then, beginning at the tip of each middle toe, he divided the skin along the bottom of the foot and up the inside of the leg just to the point where the leg joins the body.

With a sharp knife, working at the edges of the

first cut, he removed the skin from the body until he reached the legs. These he separated from the body at hips and shoulders, taking care not to cut the skin. With the leg and foot bones still inside their pocket of skin, his knife continued on around the body until, working from both sides toward the backbone, it was completely removed. Then he cut the head off at the neck, again without cutting the skin. Carefully working the skin off the legs and head, he removed as much flesh as he possibly could without removing the bones of the legs, feet and skull.

When the skin was as clean as he could get it, he placed it in a strong salt-water bath kept in a large barrel on the forward part of the boat. He would leave it there for twenty-four to thirty hours. After that he would take it out and rub the inside and the attached bones thoroughly with arsenical soap. Next he would sprinkle powdered alum all over to absorb moisture. Finally he would hang the skin up and leave it to dry in the wind and, if possible, the shade. There was little shade on the deck of the boat, so he solved that problem by hanging the skins from the mast and taking them down during the middle of the day, when the sun was hottest. When the skins were finally dry, he would take them down, fold them up as carefully as if each were a Sunday coat, and pack them up to send back to Rochester.

In all he got twenty-six crocodiles on the Jumna near Etawah, and did some successful hunting in the nearby hills, too. Then, having been in this part of India for two months, he decided to move on.

4
A Year in the Jungle

Hornaday got his first chance at really big game in the Wainaad Forest in southern India. Here were Indian bison and deer. A few days after his arrival he got his first bison.

He had left his camp early in the morning, with three natives to aid him. At two in the afternoon they struck the fresh trail of a solitary bull and followed it rapidly for some time. The bull started running and they chased it through the jungle, across a dry gully, and up a hill. Then they spotted their prey again, quietly walking along about eighty yards away. One shot at his heart region and he sank to his knees, but he was up again in an instant and heading for a thicket. Running and reloading at the same time, Hornaday came up to where the bull had been standing when first struck. The bison dashed out of the thicket and started running. A shot into his shoulders and he staggered, lost his balance, and fell over on his back, rolling down the hill into the bottom of the gully. A last bullet into his heart "saved the noble animal at least some minutes of suffering," his slayer wrote in his diary.

The Animallai Hill country was Hornaday's next hunting ground. "Animallai" literally means "Elephant Mountains," and it was a most appropriate name for the hunter's paradise he found. He was truly in his element here, in splendid open forests where herds of elephants, bison, axis deer, wild hogs, Indian elk, ibis, and more seemed to be his for the asking. He even had hopes of meeting up with tiger, leopard, or bear.

But most of all he was looking forward to what he knew was the grandest and most exciting of all field sports, hunting elephants. At the very least he wanted one skin and two skeletons to send home. He had greater fear of and respect for the elephant, which he called the true king of beasts, than any other wild animal he was acquainted with. Hunting elephants would require all the endurance, perseverance, coolness, good judgment, and knowledge of an animal's habits he could bring to the job.

It would not be too hard to get up close enough to get a shot: the elephant's poor senses of smell and hearing took care of that. The problem would be to get his bullet right into the brain, surrounded as it was by the mass of bone and flesh that made up the animal's huge head. He'd have to stalk his prey until he could get in position in front of it at about twenty paces or less. Then he could fire into the brain. The slightest accident or mistake would place him within the power of the terrible trunk, and then the huge knees or forefeet would be upon his chest crushing him to death. He had heard of hunters escaping alive from the very jaws of lions, tigers, leopards, and bears. But he had never heard of a man who fell into the clutches of an infuriated wild elephant and lived to tell the story.

He fully appreciated the challenge.

The very day after his arrival in the Animallai Hills he and his native trackers followed an elephant trail for more than an hour. Then they finally came upon a herd of sixteen grazing on some young bamboo shoots. His eye fell immediately on the oldest and largest of the herd. Patiently he stalked around and through the herd while the old tusker wandered along a hillside, feeding, not sensing the approaching danger. Carefully watching it as it lazily and leisurely moved about, swinging its huge trunk from side to side, he waited for a chance at a good shot.

Coming to a clump of bamboo, the tusker chose a tender young shoot from the very center of the clump. Hornaday thought it looked very much like a huge stalk of asparagus, twenty feet high. The elephant wrapped his trunk around the chosen shoot, stepped back, and pulled it out. He crushed it into pieces with his forefeet before bringing it up to his mouth.

Eventually the herd began to wander away from the hillside, leaving slowly in small groups. Three of them started off, followed by the one on which Hornaday had set his heart. They were walking in single file. Hornaday moved away too, keeping parallel to them behind a thicket of jungle plants. When the first one reached a bamboo clump Hornaday crouched down on the other side of it, less than twenty feet away, to watch them go past. This might be his chance.

His chosen target was last in line. When the third beast walked past the clump Hornaday got his rifle into position. He waited eagerly, looking out from behind a bamboo cover. Slowly his tusker pushed through the thorny tangle. He was now only fifteen feet away. Taking careful aim at the ear opening, Hornaday fired and sprang back behind the bamboo to be out of the way when the beast fell.

But the tusker never fell! He threw up his trunk, gave a thrilling shriek, and rushed off trumpeting through the forest! The shot had been a failure, and the hunter couldn't figure out why or how.

Later he figured what had gone wrong. He had been kneeling when he aimed, and the bullet passed above his mark because he had not taken into account the angle from which he was shooting. If he had aimed ten inches lower he would have had his elephant.

For six weeks he devoted himself to elephants, and still he got none. There were a few more inexplicable misses, but many days passed without sight of a herd. And many more days passed while he wrestled with jungle fever, which sooner or later came to all travelers in that part of the world. Fortunately he had brought his quinine, and soon he was well enough to go back to work. Then, with a tiger hunt, his luck changed for the better.

It happened late one morning while he was out

tracking elephants. Coming to a dry, sandy riverbed he discovered what his native aides assured him was the fresh trail of a large tiger. They followed the trail for about a mile. Suddenly Pera Vera, his chief tracker, gripped him fiercely by the arm and pointed to a spot about thirty yards distant.

Hornaday looked where the tracker had pointed.

"It's Old Stripes sure enough," he said to himself, and then, "Great Caesar! He's as big as an ox! Just look at how those black stripes gleam in the sun!"

His chance to shoot came when the tiger paused in the middle of the stream, facing them. He aimed at the left eye and fired, and without even stopping to see the results reloaded his rifle. He expected the wounded beast to charge, possibly attacking one of the men. If so, he would put his next bullet through the tiger's brain.

Ready to shoot, he looked around for the tiger, and by signs Pera Vera told him it was still in the same place. It was turning slowly around and around, its head tilting to one side, indicating a wound in its left eye. The shot had been perfect! One more shot broke the spinal cord, and the tiger dropped silently to the sand, gasping, kicking, and foaming at the mouth. In three minutes he was dead.

Then the hunter had his moment of triumph, the moment when he first put his hand upon the fallen game. Hornaday savored the pleasure of handling the cruel teeth and knife-like claws that, only minutes before, had been so dangerous. He stroked the body while it was still warm, and touched the feet that had made the tracks.

His first tiger! And what a tiger it was! Fully 9 feet 8½ inches from the tip of the nose to the end of the tail; the tail alone was three and a half feet long. It weighed nearly 500 pounds, and Hornaday wrote in his diary that it was "just in the prime of tiger-hood, fat, sleek, and glossy."

Three weeks after the tiger he had another chance at the elusive elephants, and this time he was successful. But what a job it was to skeletonize an elephant! He and half a dozen helpers camped near where the beast had fallen, for it would have been impossible to bring it to their camp.

Fortunately it had fallen over on its side, so measuring it was easy. It was 8 feet 4 inches high at the shoulders; the top of the carcass came up as high as Hornaday's chin, and the hunter was not a short man. He felt as though he were quarrying the bones out of a mountain of flesh and blood. He started to strip away the skin, as he had done for the crocodiles. When he cut the two upper legs off, he put two men to work removing the flesh. The strength of both of them was needed just to roll one foreleg over.

Their work took two full days; but finally it was done. He saved the skin of all four feet to make into footstools, and he also saved the tail as a trophy.

He still wanted another elephant, but they were hard to come by. Axis deer and black monkeys, however, were common in the vicinity. If he had wanted to, he could have shot deer by the dozen, but he never shot one that was not needed for its skin, skeleton, or venison. Hating to see game slaughtered for no purpose, he killed only about twenty, which he considered a modest number. Hornaday had great hatred for the sort of game-butchers who were at that very time killing off nearly all of the bison in the western states and territories of the United States. Some time later when he himself was in good bison-hunting territory, he carefully restricted the number he shot.

He got the largest of his bison bulls quite early one morning and decided to skin it on the spot. When this was done the skin was slung over a pole, and it made a heavy load even for four men to carry.

Back at camp, the rest of the day was spent in preparing it. The skin was very thick, and it had to be pared down and scraped on the inside until the roots of the hair could be seen. Only then would his preservatives be able to do their work. This was a tedious and painstaking job, done with thin-bladed and very sharp knives by his native helpers under his direction. By late afternoon he was ready to rub the inside of the skin with his arsenical soap. The next step would have been soaking it in salt water, which was the way the crocodile and other skins had been treated. But it was too big. So he sprinkled it with twelve pounds of very coarse salt, rubbing this in vigorously with flat stones. Then his men rolled the skin up for the night. The next morning they thinned it down some more, sprinkled about eight pounds of alum over it, rubbing it in well, and left it lying on the ground for several hours. After that Hornaday hung it up over a pole in the shade to dry. At night he would take it down, fold it up, and put it inside his hut to keep it from the evening dew and rain. After one rainy day, two sunny days, and one day that was merely damp, the skin was dry enough to pack.

But the work of preparing and drying that bison skin was nothing compared to what lay ahead when he shot his next elephant. It had taken days to find the herd, hours to stalk it. He had only an instant in which to shoot, but this time his aim was perfect. He floored the nine-foot beast with a single shot that passed clean through the skull and brain, burying itself ten inches deep in the thick flesh of the neck. In celebration he climbed right up on top of the carcass and cheered loudly!

With five native helpers he set about to measure and skin his prize. Although it was almost night, they went to work at once. The skin was so large that he decided to remove it in three pieces, instead of one as with every other skin. He would cut into it in such a way that, when stuffed and mounted, none of the taxidermist's seams would show. He cut off the head just at the crease in the neck. Then he divided the skin in the middle of the back, a job he called "terrible work" because the skin was so thick—$1\frac{1}{2}$ inches —and tough. He was glad he had had such good knives made for him in England.

By the time the uppermost side of the elephant was fully skinned, it was quite late. He and his men washed in a nearby stream, built a campfire, and ate some rice for dinner. He slung his hammock between two trees.

The natives sat around the campfire chattering, while he swung gently to and fro above them, looking out at the large jungle leaves gleaming in the firelight. The night was clear, there was a soft breeze from the west, and they were the only human beings for miles around. Surveying the scene with satisfaction, he thought, "This is the jolliest life that was ever led."

The next day it took him and the men two hours just to roll the carcass over so they could work on the other side of the skin. When they had it off they spread both skin pieces out, insides facing up, and covered them and the head with green boughs to shield them from the sun. Then they returned to camp. They would bring preservatives and a tent and provisions back with them to finish the job of curing the skin on the spot.

When the skin pieces and head were ready for preservatives, he treated them much the same as he had those of the bison. Then came the job of cleaning the bones.

The day after that was Hornaday's birthday. It was his second birthday since leaving home. He had been in India almost a year. Happy that the skin was safe, he took the day off and celebrated.

5
Stuffed Animals

His next birthday found him in Sarawak on the island of Borneo. The year just passed had seen many more adventures. Flying foxes and anteaters, giant turtles and slender gibbons, orangutans, queer-looking dugongs, and giant snakes had crossed his path. He had visited the house where a head-hunting tribe of Dyaks kept their trophies. "The heads, or rather skulls, hang in a semi-circle around one side of the room, and there are forty-two of them in all," he wrote in his journal. "The collection as a whole is in very good condition, the specimens being moderately clean and not at all smoked. Some have been very carelessly taken, I regret to say, as is shown by the way they are split open or slashed across with parongs (knives); and from some, large pieces have been hacked out." Half in jest, the scientist noted that "none of the skulls is labeled with locality, date, sex, and species, as crania always should be, to be valuable."

Before coming to Borneo he had gone hunting on the Malay Peninsula, and before that he had spent three months in Ceylon, following instructions from Professor Ward.

"Plunder Ceylon," the Professor had written. "Rake the island over as with a fine-toothed comb; catch everything you can, and send me the best of it."

His headquarters in Colombo, the chief city of Ceylon, were two ground-floor rooms opening on a paved patio. Here he received the dozen or so natives he had sent out to gather specimens that he would buy. In just one day he listed the following items: three soft-shelled turtles, one tortoise, forty-nine crabs of three different kinds, fifteen sea cockroaches, twelve green lizards, four ordinary lizards, two bats, nine jumping fish, one horned skate, six fish of various species, four prawns, and about one hundred shells of many species. Each was cleaned, preserved, and labeled with its common and Latin names. The next day brought snakes of various kinds, frogs, fish, and invertebrates, all of which he shipped home to Rochester.

Now at last he was winding up his jungle tours and beginning the long return journey, "Never has a country used me better or sent me away fuller handed," he said when he sailed from Sarawak to Singapore two weeks later. "It's too bad I didn't have a score of friends here to enjoy it with me."

He regretted leaving, but he was glad to be on his way home. He would be seeing Josephine again, the young woman he would soon marry.

In April of 1879 he was back in Rochester. Only a few hours after his return he presented to Professor Ward a sketch of a mounted animal display that he wished to prepare, a sketch based upon a group of orangutans he had seen fighting viciously in the tree-tops in Borneo. The sketch was revolutionary: Several animals were to be mounted together, not just standing, but in a setting that was to be a copy of an actual section of a real forest. There were to be two large male orangs fighting, a female orang with a baby clinging to her breast, looking for a safer and higher perch, and a young orang looking down from a nest in a higher tree.

Such a group had never been done before. Until that time specimens had been mounted alone or, if in groups, standing still, never posed as in real life, and never engaged in real activity. But in his years of observing jungle life as it really was, Hornaday had determined to change all that.

Unlike most taxidermists, he had seen with his own eyes how wild animals really walk, stand, run. He had even taught himself to sketch so he could record the scenes he came upon, and preserve for himself the way an animal looked and what it did in its own home or natural habitat. No longer would he pose a mounted specimen from someone else's drawing in a book. After all, that artist probably had never seen what he was drawing.

He couldn't wait to get started.

Since coming to Ward's, he had proved to the stern professor that he knew what he was talking about. He had certainly gotten results on all of his field trips, even the first. And the collections he had made on this last trip were truly astounding. So, although these ideas were new to him, Ward gave him permission to go ahead with his project.

From April to September he worked on his orang group. He was so busy with it that he waited until its completion, in September, to marry his "guardian angel."

He gave his display, which was complete with the necessary jungle foliage, a title: "Fight in the Treetops." While working on it he had also written a scientific paper about the orangutans of Borneo. Ward was so pleased he sent the "Fight" group to the American Association for the Advancement of Science, to be shown at its annual meeting. Hornaday went along too, to read his paper.

One of the scientists present was Professor George Brown Goode, Assistant Secretary of the Smithsonian Institution in Washington. Then and there he offered the twenty-five-year-old Hornaday the position, vacant at the time, of chief taxidermist to the Smithsonian's United States National Museum. But Hornaday would not leave Rochester until he finished working on the specimens he had collected. He also planned to write a book, based on his journal, about his adventures.

His fellow-workers at Ward's were inspired by this new approach. With Hornaday as the leader, Ward's became the focal point of a new movement in taxidermy. That winter he proposed that they form an organization to attract attention to their new methods, and to improve the quality of museum exhibits throughout the country. In his and Josephine's Rochester home the Society of American Taxidermists was founded. Frederick S. Webster, who specialized in bird mounting (Hornaday called him a wizard at it), was elected president. Hornaday himself asked for, and got, the job of secretary. He wanted to correspond with other members of the profession and with zoologists and naturalists so he could propagandize for the new ideas.

The society held its first exhibition in Rochester later that year. Taxidermists throughout the country were invited to submit specimens to compete for various prizes. Three museum men who were thought by the society to be sympathetic to its cause were selected as judges. Hornaday's fighting orangs won first prize. But the second prize went to a solitary woodduck on a pedestal.

They were all disappointed, and no one more so than Frederick Webster, the duck's creator. For in giving it the prize the judges had overlooked his other entry. This was a realistic group of three flamingoes, two standing at the edge of a real-looking lagoon, the third sitting on a mud nest nearby. Webster had made it painstakingly, in his free time after work at Ward's, and at his own expense. The other charter members of the society considered it to be an excellent example of the kind of taxidermy they wanted to do. They had all been rooting for it.

When the judges further declared that dramatic

groups of animals such as Hornaday's were not suitable for display in scientific museums, the group's disappointment was complete.

They were somewhat encouraged that the American Museum of Natural History in New York had ordered a large group to be mounted by Hornaday, to be called "The Orangutan at Home." But they knew it would be many years before the museums and the public were convinced. The society had plenty of work to do.

By the time the society was ready for its third exhibition, held in New York in 1883, Hornaday had taken Dr. Goode's offer and was Chief Taxidermist at the National Museum. The "Fight In the Treetops" had been bought from Professor Ward by the Smithsonian Institution for the museum, and had followed Hornaday to Washington. Now his work was displayed before the whole nation. It was a beginning, and an opportunity. If only the public would respond, showing a preference for such groups over the lifeless displays shown everywhere else.

The week before the New York exhibition was to open, one of the sponsors, who had promised $500 toward the expenses of renting space, backed out and broke his word. The taxidermists were in a fix, and Hornaday considered himself responsible.

Fortunately he recalled that Andrew Carnegie, whom he had met during his East Indies trip, was at that very moment in New York. Hurriedly packing a valise, he left Washington to call upon the millionaire.

With all the eloquence he could muster, he explained the program and purposes of the society, and how useful his group was going to be in developing the museums of the United States. Hesitantly, he asked for a loan of $500, to be repaid when the society could afford it.

"What?" asked Mr. Carnegie. "Is five hundred dollars *all* you need?"

Blushing, the representative of American taxidermy admitted that it was.

"Well," came the welcome response, "I will give you that, and you need not bother to return it!"

This unexpected generosity led Hornaday to propose that Carnegie be made the society's treasurer for a year, and he was surprised that the famous industrialist did not even laugh at the suggestion. Instead, he gravely accepted, and for that year the group's financial standing was, as its executive secretary proudly stated, "as solid as the Rock of Gibraltar." This was the first, but not the last, time that Hornaday would enlist Carnegie in the cause of zoology.

His mounted young African elephant, Mungo, won first prize at the competition. And this was a triumph for another new idea. During the months and years that he had been abroad collecting skins and skeletons, he had also been gathering ideas about what to do with them. When he butchered animals he had seen how the muscles fit into the flesh, and how the bones shape the body. When he mounted his animals he would not make puffy-looking faces or round, club-like legs, arms, and fingers. In the field he had realized how ridiculous the round legs and straw-filled bodies looked, compared to the real thing. He would build up his mounted animals as nature built them in life. He would construct a skeleton first. If the animals' own bones and skull were handy he would use them; if not, he would teach himself to carve duplicates out of wood. For the fleshy part of the body he wanted some material that would hold its shape. The tow or straw that other taxidermists were using was all wrong. So was the way they packed it into the skin. Their animals had hard barrel-like bodies at first; after a year or so they sagged, bulged, got limp, and *looked stuffed*. His, he resolved, would look real, alive. He would breathe new life into stuffed animals!

Mungo was the ultimate test of the new method. Hornaday had first built a skeleton-like structure called a manikin, and then covered it with an enormous quantity of clay before shaping the skin on it. This was his solution to the problem of shaping the animal's body realistically. And the prize vindicated his efforts.

This was not the only innovation unveiled in New York that year. Until this time mounted mammals were displayed without any kind of background whatever. Although bird displays were given a background treatment, only a suggestion of the natural surroundings was made: this was usually a watercolor representation of sky and clouds. But now Hornaday showed his display against a setting realistically painted and complete down to the last detail. This had never been attempted anywhere before. And the fact that he was showing not only birds but also a mammal against such a background made it all the more startling. His effort showed a white setter dog pointing a covey of bobwhite quail—the dog was obviously about to lead a hunter to the game. He had hired an artist to paint a complete landscape, showing the country—the environment—in which the dog and birds lived.

"Coming to the Point" won a prize, but in the special category of ornamental taxidermy. He was disappointed, for he had hoped, as a result of his work, to gain acceptance for painted backgrounds in museum displays.

His disappointment would last for a long time. Even ten years later he would sadly comment, "As yet the museums will have no painted backgrounds." But he predicted that some day they would, and that then they would be "as attractive and pleasing as the picture galleries."

He lived to see it come true. And his efforts, and those of his colleagues, helped. Dr. Goode helped, too. It was Dr. Goode's idea to give credit to both the taxidermist and the background artist by including their names on the museum labels. But most of all the public helped, by recognizing the difference and responding to it.

Hornaday himself became known to the public after publication of his book, *Two Years in the Jungle*. Readers enjoyed his adventures, and absorbed jungle lore through his observant eyes. Boys read it, and decided to become naturalists or hunters when they grew up.

The book was dedicated to "My Good Wife Josephine."

6
The Near Extermination of the American Bison

As Chief Taxidermist of the National Museum, Hornaday's job was to plan and produce animal exhibits. One day early in 1886 he realized that in the museum belonging to the entire nation there was not a single American bison display that met his own high standards.

He could not say when he had first become concerned with *bison Americanus*, or buffalo as it is more familiarly called. Perhaps it was during his first winter at Ward's, when a load of fresh buffalo skins arrived from Wyoming, and he and the other workers spent a week working on the thick, shaggy hides. Perhaps it was in the cities and jungles of India, where the beast of burden, with its tough hide and patchy hair, seemed to him ugly in comparison with its majestic cousin in his native land.

He took inventory at the museum: one mounted

female skin, another unmounted, and two old, delapidated, and poorly mounted skins. In addition there were: one complete male skeleton, an incomplete skeleton, a few broken skulls, and two mounted heads. There was not even one presentable male of good size, typical of the species.

He had to get new display specimens. But time was running out. These animals which had been plentiful only twenty years earlier were being slaughtered at a fantastic rate. If he waited too much longer, there might be no more bison for him to preserve.

He planned his course of action. First he needed specific details. How many buffalo were left? How many had there once been, for that matter? And where might the surviving animals be found? He wrote to everyone he could think of—hunters, soldiers, travelers, postmasters, ranchers—in the land that had been buffalo country only a short while ago.

When the answers to his letters began to come back, he was stunned. He had known that the animal millions were going, but now he realized with a start that they were almost gone!

He pieced the story together from the scattered reports that came in to him.

Between 1800 and 1870 the country west of the Mississippi River was one vast buffalo range. The animals lived and moved in huge multitudes, like grand armies passing in review. They interfered with travelers and settlers. They frequently stopped boats on the rivers. They derailed locomotives and railroad cars.

In 1871 a Colonel Dodge, traveling in a light wagon

between two forts only 34 miles apart on the Arkansas River, drove 25 miles through an immense buffalo herd. He wrote afterward, "The whole country appeared one great mass of buffalo." Other travelers in the area reported that the same herd took five days to pass a given point. Colonel Dodge calculated that the herd extended for as much as 25 by 50 miles, and that he had seen half a million beasts in a single day!

And that was only a fraction of the buffalo population in the United States and Canada. From reports like these Hornaday was able to estimate that in 1868 there had been six million. And there may have been more. Now, less than twenty years later, there were perhaps six hundred.

Between 1865 and 1869 the Union Pacific Railroad was built, spanning the continent and cutting the buffalo herd into two parts. The railroad, and the branch lines that began to sprout from it, brought men and breech-loading long-range repeating rifles right into buffalo country. As towns became settled in the newly opened-up portions of the country, they became headquarters for hunters. There was a market, back east, for buffalo robes.

The southern portion of the herd was the first to go. It was systematically plundered from 1871 on. By 1875 only scattered bands of buffalo remained. During the first three years of slaughter, between three and five animals were killed and wasted for every hide that reached the market.

There was a market for buffalo meat, too. The tongue, preserved in salt, was a particular delicacy. Hornaday believed that at least 50,000 animals had

been slaughtered for their tongues alone. A man might bring in two barrels of tongues, and not another part of the buffalo—not a pound of meat, not even the robe. It was easier to cut out a tongue than to skin an animal and then cure the hide.

When there were no buffalo left south of the transcontinental railroad, the hunters went north, into the Dakotas, Montana, Wyoming. In Montana one hunter killed one hundred and seven animals in one hour, without changing his position. That hunter accounted for about five thousand in a season. And there were five thousand hunters and skinners trying to do the same.

The great destruction had begun while Hornaday was in college. That was just a dozen years before. More than three and a half million head of buffalo on the southern range had been killed, close to two million in the north. There were absolutely no state, territorial, or national governmental limitations on the slaughter. No one had thought, seeing the vast herds, that the supply of buffalo would ever be diminished. And no one really cared. No one, until Hornaday.

He prepared a memorandum showing the extent of the destruction that had already taken place. He pointed out that this was truly the National Museum's last chance to get specimens, if indeed it wasn't too late already. His memorandum was addressed to Professor Spencer Fullerton Baird, head of the Smithsonian Institution, and to Dr. Goode.

Professor Baird sent for him immediately. He had

had no idea that the bison were that near to total destruction.

"I am greatly shocked and disturbed by your letter," he said. "I dislike being the means of killing any of these last bison, but since it is now utterly impossible to prevent their destruction, we simply must go after specimens. You must go west as soon as possible, and find out if specimens can still be obtained. If it is not too late, collect twenty or thirty skins, the same number of skeletons, and pick up about fifty skulls." Hornaday had reported that bones and skulls were simply lying about, bleaching in the sun, where the buffalo carcasses had rotted.

Professor Baird continued. "We must get enough specimens not only for ourselves, but for the other museums that will need them too. The Smithsonian will meet the expenses. I will ask the Secretaries of War and the Interior to help us."

Baird, Goode, and Hornaday all felt terrible about killing twenty or thirty animals. But they were convinced that, even if they did not, the species would still not survive.

Of the less than three hundred buffalo then believed to be still alive in the United States more than half were in Montana. The rest were scattered in Dakota, Texas, and Colorado. Hornaday decided to try Montana first.

The Smithsonian's call for help was quickly answered. The Secretary of War directed that forts in the area to which Hornaday was going furnish him with field transportation, military escort, and camp equipment. He also directed the forts to sell Hornaday supplies from their commissaries. The Secretary of the Interior, meanwhile, directed all of its scouts, Indian agents, and other employees to cooperate with Hornaday if called upon.

On May 6 Hornaday left Washington, heading for Miles City, Montana. With him was his assistant taxidermist, A. H. Forney, and his friend George H. Hedley of Medina, New York.

Just before he left, an acquaintance of his, a retired army captain, had visited him in his laboratory.

"Well," began the captain. "I hear you're going to Montana to hunt buffalo. I'll bet you a hundred dollars that you don't find even one wild one."

Hornaday was not a gambling man. But he hoped the captain's information was wrong.

On May 9 they arrived at Fort Keogh, near Miles City. They stayed here a few days, making inquiries, organizing the equipment for the hunt.

No one knew of any wild buffalo anywhere. "There *are* no more buffalo." "You can't get buffalo any more." These words were repeated by everyone to whom he spoke.

He was discouraged.

Then he met Henry R. Phillips, owner of the LU-bar Ranch, and he knew he had come to the right place. "Certainly there are a few buffalo in the badlands west of my place," Phillips told him. "One of our cowboys killed a cow a few weeks ago; and about thirty-five head have been seen. If you go up there and hunt them—and stick to it—you're almost sure to get some."

On May 13 they set out. In addition to Hornaday and his two assistants, the party included a five-man military escort, a cook, and a teamster. The army had also provided a six-mule team, and gear for the two saddle horses he had bought in Miles City.

They traveled slowly through dry, treeless country. On the third day they came to the first bleaching bones of a buffalo. Once this region had been a famous buffalo range. Now the dry, white skeletons lay thickly on the trail, ghastly monuments to slaughter. They lay precisely as they had fallen years before, the heads stretched forward as if gasping their last. They saw more than thirty skeletons in little more than an acre: here a hunter undoubtedly had gotten a "stand" on a "bunch" and picked them off from behind the rocks. Hornaday selected three of the finest, largest complete skeletons.

A few days later they reached the LU-bar Ranch, about eighty miles northwest of Miles City. They found a Cheyenne Indian to serve as a scout and guide; and occasionally they were able to enlist the services of a cowboy who was familiar with the region. Each day they would ride over the country, covering a new section of it.

One day they found a buffalo calf that had been unable to keep up with its mother and had been separated from the herd. When the calf saw them riding toward it, it started to run. But it was weak, and they caught up with it in a few minutes. They jumped off their horses and tried to catch it in their arms, but the calf butted first one and then another. It even butted the mule. Finally a cowboy had to lasso it.

Now they had a marvelous living specimen to take back with them.

Ten days later two bull buffaloes were sighted, and one of them was killed. Its skin was in bad condition: it was shedding its heavy winter growth of hair and the new hair was patchy and uneven. They took the skeleton, but the skin of the head and neck only.

Hornaday knew that there was indeed a herd here, but decided it would be better to wait until autumn so that animals with a good growth of hair could be taken. He planned to return to Washington.

On September 24 Hornaday was again in Miles City; his only assistant was W. Harvey Brown, a senior student at the University of Kansas. Three cowboys were waiting to guide and hunt with him. They purchased two months' supply of foodstuffs, and rented horses and a light ranch wagon. The cowboys provided their own mounts. In all there were ten horses in their outfit: a team to draw the wagon, and two for each hunter. The worst problem of provisions was hauling enough grain for ten hard-working horses. They took 2000 pounds of oats.

Shortly after sunrise on October 14, they picked up a bison trail and followed it south. It led out of the butte country where they had been until now, and into a new and difficult terrain. The dry soil was loose and crumbling, and the horses' hooves sank deep into it at every step. They struggled through a thick growth of sagebrush. Finally the bdlands ended and they followed the trail into grassy country, but here they could not make out the tracks. At noon they paused on a high point, and with binoculars discovered fourteen buffalo about two miles away.

They crept up to within 200 yards and fired, but missed. After a chase, Hornaday and one of the cowboys killed two each.

Two days later, on the same spot, the cowboys got four more. The largest of them fell late in the afternoon at some distance from their camp. There was not enough daylight left to do a complete skinning job, so the cowboys partly skinned the legs, dressed the carcass to preserve the meat, and left it there, planning, to come back the next day to finish the job.

In the morning they discovered that Piegan Indians had beaten them to it. The skin and the edible meat were all gone; even the leg-bones had been cracked for the marrow. They had not skinned the head, but it was useless for zoological purposes now. One side of it was covered with red warpaint, the other with yellow.

By the twentieth of November, exactly two months since Hornaday had left Washington, the party had bagged twenty animals, the minimum number hoped for.

That night it started to snow, a real Montana blizzard that lasted a full week. Fortunately their camp was well sheltered, between the rocky walls of a canyon, protected by an overhanging bluff. They passed the time telling buffalo stories and hunting yarns, throwing wood into their camp stove, and feeding oats to their horses. By December 6 the snow had melted enough for them to go out. Hornaday and one of the cowboys rode off on a last trip for buffalo.

They found three, an enormous old bull, an adult cow, and a two-year-old heifer. Hornaday shot the bull through the shoulder, breaking the foreleg, and it dropped to the ground. Then, one more shot and the bull was dead.

It was a particularly magnificent specimen, larger than any other they had taken, or heard of, for that matter. Its hair was in excellent condition, long, thick, evenly and richly colored. Hornaday estimated the old bull's weight at 1600 pounds.

The last buffalo hunt was successful, and he could leave Montana having completed his mission.

About a week later they left, and five days after that reached Miles City, just ahead of a snowstorm which had been threatening for days. Hornaday and Brown spent the next snowbound days packing up and organizing their collection. It filled twenty-one large cases, which eventually reached the museum in good condition.

The new year had just begun when the party returned to Washington. A year had passed since Hornaday first thought of going after *bison Americanus*. Now they would begin preparing and mounting the specimens, planning the setting in which he would place them. Hornaday wanted a group that would show buffalo of all ages. It would be a monument to a vanished native species.

The job of stuffing and mounting the specimens took over a year. The group included six buffaloes: a cow, a young bull, a young cow, and a yearling as well as a baby calf and an old bull. Hornaday planned to use some bleached buffalo skulls and a few fossil bones, too. A large mahogany and glass case, 16 feet long by 12 feet wide and 10 feet high, had been built to his specifications.

Everything was brought into the south end of the south hall of the museum. Shielded by screens from the curious gaze of the public, Hornaday and his two assistants worked to install the group in the case. Only one outsider, a reporter from the *Washington Star*, was allowed to watch them as they put the finishing touches on what Hornaday hoped would be his taxidermic masterpiece.

On March 10, 1888, two days before the bison group was to be unveiled, a newspaper headline caught his eye.

"A SCENE FROM MONTANA—SIX OF MR. HORNADAY'S BUFFALOES FORM A PICTURESQUE GROUP—A BIT OF THE WILD WEST REPRODUCED AT THE NATIONAL MUSEUM—SOMETHING NOVEL IN THE WAY OF TAXIDERMY—REAL BUFFALO-GRASS, REAL MONTANA DIRT, AND REAL BUFFALOES."

He began to read.

"A little bit of Montana—a small square patch from the wildest part of the wild West—has been transferred to the National Museum. It is so little that Montana will never miss it, but enough to enable one who has the faintest glimmer of imagination to see it all for himself—the hummocky prairie, the buffalo-grass, the sagebrush, and the buffalo. It is as though a little group of buffalo that have come to drink at a pool had been suddenly struck motionless by some magic spell, each in a natural attitude, and then the section of prairie, pool, buffalo, and all had been carefully cut out and brought to the National Museum.

"The group, with its accessories, has been prepared so as to tell in an attractive way to the general visitor to the Museum the story of the buffalo, but care has been taken at the same time to secure an accuracy of detail that will satisfy the critical scrutiny of the most technical naturalist. It represents a new departure in mounting specimens for museums. The American mammals collected by Mr. Hornaday will be mounted in a manner that will make each piece or group an object lesson telling something of the history and habits of the animal."

He was delighted. That reporter who had been snooping about while he worked had understood what he was trying to do. The public would, too.

With the bison group finished and cordially received, he had a double accomplishment of which to be proud. He had convincingly demonstrated that the new taxidermy belonged in museums, as a dramatic tool for educating the public. And he had preserved in the nation's capital city its grandest and most distinctive animal.

Good. Now he could get on with his next project. It was already taking shape in his mind.

7
Zoo Building

The year before, while designing his bison group and processing the spoils of his Montana campaign, Hornaday had had an inspiration. The nation must have a national zoo. In Washington. At once. It could provide a home for a small herd of buffaloes. They could breed and perpetuate the species in peace. Why had no one thought of it before?

No one had. No one had even noticed that while all major cities in Europe had their zoological gardens, the capital city of the United States had none. The oldest city zoo in America had been in existence less than twenty years. And only four or five other cities had started zoos of their own since then.

In May, 1887, Hornaday wrote a letter to Professor Baird proposing the founding of a National Zoological Garden.

The reply came a few hours later. Dr. Goode came to see him. "I have here your letter proposing a National Zoological Garden for Washington," he began. "It is a very good idea."

His enthusiasm rising, Hornaday began to speak. But his friend and colleague stopped him. "Unfortunately, as you know, Professor Baird is a very sick man," Dr. Goode said. "We'll have to put this aside for now. Later, we can discuss it."

Hornaday went back to his bison. He was writing a paper about the animal. He wrote of the long history of the buffalo, about where in America it had once lived, about its majestic appearance, its life cycle, and its possible uses to man. He told in chilling detail the sad story of its near extinction. And he wrote of the last bison hunt, in which he had played a leading part. Two articles by him were published that year in *Cosmopolitan* magazine.

In the summer Professor Baird died. Shortly after that Dr. Goode created a Department of Living Animals in the National Museum. Hornaday was to be its curator. They planned to build a little tryout zoo on the Smithsonian grounds, to test the public interest. But first they had to get some wild animals to Washington.

In September Dr. Goode was made Acting United States Fish Commissioner, in addition to his other jobs. It was then that he found a way to get some animals. The Fish Commission was sending a railroad car containing large metal tanks full of fish into the western states and territories. They would try to stock lakes and ponds with carp. Hornaday would go along. As the fish were delivered to their destinations, he would fill the empty tanks with whatever animals he could capture en route.

So they set out. In Seattle, Portland, Salt Lake City, and other western cities, with their surrounding countryside, he gathered as many living animals as the car could hold, and more. The car became so crowded that his sleeping berth was right on top of a badger.

In early November they paused in Cheyenne, Wyoming. The railroad car, loaded with wild beasts, stayed on a siding at the station while fish were delivered to ranchers in the vicinity. News of its contents raced through the town. People left their homes and their work to come to the railroad station.

"Please, may we see the animals?" they would ask. "We have never seen any wild animals!"

Hornaday was astounded. "They are as hungry to see some wild western beasts as if none ever existed outside of this railroad car," he thought. "My goodness! And these are the people who settled the West! Imagine what city people back east will say!"

He realized then how the settlements had driven the larger mammals from all but the most remote parts of the country. It was certainly high time for somebody to build a national zoo!

In temporary wooden structures and wire corrals, the menagerie was established on the lawn to the west of the Smithsonian's main building. As soon as it became known that there were over two hundred wild animals in Washington, visitors flocked to see them.

Two bison were presented by a New Yorker, and an

Indian agent on the Sioux Reservation donated five more. These formed the first United States National Bison Herd.

Hornaday was delighted. His new little zoo was making possible this first governmental attempt to breed buffalo, keeping them from the rapid extinction that had all but overtaken them. It showed what could be done, what *should* be done.

By now the Smithsonian Institution had its new Secretary, Professor S. P. Langley. Hornaday called him "that austere physicist from Pittsburgh." The crowds that came to see Hornaday's animals were right beneath Langley's window, and he could hardly keep from being impressed at their interest in living specimens. Soon he began to be quite concerned with the plans for a zoo that Hornaday and Goode were busy drawing up.

Goode had suggested a location for the zoo in the beautiful Rock Creek area. Three prominent senators were interested in sponsoring a bill that would permit land to be acquired. The Senate appropriated $200,000 immediately. Then Hornaday was assigned to lobby to get the bill passed by the House of Representatives.

He made a model of the proposed site, a relief map built to scale. He put on it a forest of miniature trees and every other feature of the hundred and sixty-six picturesque acres they had chosen. For two sessions he explained the project to members of Congress, and urged them to vote in its favor.

By that time his paper on the buffalo was complete. It was published in the *Annual Report* of the Smithsonian Institution. It was called "The Extermination of the American Bison."

Secretary Langley, as chief executive of the Smithsonian Institution, was in charge of the National Zoological Park. Hornaday was its superintendent.

Dr. Langley proved to be a difficult man to work with. He had a domineering temper, and the geniality, as Hornaday put it, of an iceberg. Nevertheless, Hornaday had managed, by being diplomatic and competent, to get along well enough with him. It was even rumored, among the museum staff, that Hornaday was the only man there who was not afraid of Langley.

Hornaday spent a full year acquiring the land that had been selected for the zoo. When that was done, he drew up plans and a budget for the first year of the zoo's operation.

Then in May of 1890 a letter from Langley arrived on Hornaday's desk. It seemed clearly intended to tie his hands in developing the zoo according to the plans he had been working on. It said, in effect, that all business conducted on behalf of the Smithsonian or any of its divisions, had to be directly supervised by the Secretary. Every decision, no matter how minor, had to be cleared by the Secretary first.

Taking the bull by the horns, Hornaday made an appointment to see Langley to discuss the zoo. In the Secretary's office, he found out that Langley had, without consulting him, and not knowing the first thing himself about animals and their needs, changed around all of the plans for the layout of the zoo.

Hornaday still tried to save the situation. He proposed that Langley give him a six-month trial period to work it out his own way. Langley answered flatly, "No, Mr. Hornaday, I will *not!*"

That was that. The zoo had been Hornaday's idea from the beginning. Now it was being taken away from him, without his even being given a fair chance to try to make it work as he had envisioned it.

At home that evening he told Mrs. Hornaday about his confrontation with Dr. Langley. "And when he finally refused to give me a fair trial at it, he even stamped his foot on the carpet for emphasis!"

She saw immediately what would happen: that he would just be an animal tender for the zoo of which he was the rightful father. "There's no use in going on if you can't take satisfaction in your work," she said. "And you would only eat your heart out in disappointment."

He knew she was right. Perhaps they should leave Washington. His work here was really accomplished. The zoo would soon be established, even though not the way he had planned it. More important was his success in popularizing the new taxidermy as a result of the bison group and some others he had done. That would be his monument in Washington. He was only thirty-five years old.

"By all means, resign" said Mrs. Hornaday. "At once. We can sell this house and move to Buffalo within a month. It's just too bad that *your* zoo won't happen."

It was settled. The next day, calmly and even cheerfully, Hornaday drafted his letter of resignation. It was, as he had expected it would be, promptly accepted.

So they moved to Buffalo, New York. He took

some comfort in the name of his new city as he left wild animals and went into the real estate business. He found time, now, to fulfill a promise he had made to himself many years before. He wrote *Taxidermy and Zoological Collecting: A complete Handbook for the Amateur Taxidermist, Collector, Osteologist, Museum-builder, Sportsman, and Traveler*, which was published the next year.

Then he wrote a series of twenty articles, "The Quadrupeds of North America," for *St. Nicholas*, a popular magazine for children. He wanted young people to know, and be proud of, the fauna of their native country. The schools were not teaching them about the animals who shared the continent with them.

And then he forgot zoology altogether for a year and wrote a novel, *The Man Who Became A Savage*.

One day in 1896 he received a letter from New York City. He recognized the names on the letterhead as those of well-to-do and prominent citizens, businessmen, and lawyers well known for getting things done. They were men of the kind, as he put it, who never got involved with small things.

There was to be a New York Zoological Park, one that would be worthy of the greatest city in the hemisphere. A director was needed. His name had been suggested. Would he consider meeting with them?

His first reaction was "No, positively not." He had had enough of zoological parks. He was doing well in Buffalo.

But he really could not resist the temptation to get back to wild animals. It might be a second chance to bring the lives and personalities of thousands of interesting wild beasts within reach of millions of people. Perhaps this time he would have the chance to use his ideas of how they should be displayed.

And the city itself was a temptation. New York was the wonder city of the world; it had seemed so years ago to the Iowa farm boy. Even now, when he had been to most of the world's greatest cities, this metropolis still thrilled him.

One meeting with the members of the Zoological Society's executive committee in New York and he had the job. The city welcomed him. "DIRECTOR OF NEW YORK ZOOLOGICAL SOCIETY WELL EQUIPPED" hailed a newspaper headline.

His duties were to prepare and submit plans for the actual layout of the zoo, to build and train a working staff, to keep peace with the city and public, to inform the press, and to make all dangerous places fool-proof. Today we would say he was surveyor, architect, landscape architect, personnel manager, public relations officer, press information officer, and safety engineer.

His first task was to find a place to put the zoological park. On foot he tracked up and down through the northernmost borough of the city, the Bronx, then barely settled. In Bronx Park, with its open woods, lake, valleys, and meadows—he came upon 264 acres ideally situated. He was delighted to find a magnificent glacial boulder delicately balanced on a flat rockledge in the center of the Park. He relished the virgin forest of huge old oaks and chestnuts, tulips, sweetgums, and beeches. It seemed incredible that this could exist in New York City, undisturbed by the hand of man, until 1896! It was waiting just for him.

In two hours of wandering about he dreamed out his zoo.

He had so many ideas that he hoped to put into practice. He wanted to show his animals to the public in a setting that duplicated their natural environment as closely as possible. The birds, for instance, should have a huge enclosure to live in, complete with trees and a pond, not just small cages. He imagined a range covering acres of Bronx woodland, where the wild animals who normally lived in a cool climate, such as moose, caribou, bison, and elk, could wander, each with its own individual grazing grounds and shelter house. He wanted a prairie dog village, a beaver pond whose inhabitants could build their own dam, bear dens built with natural rock walls. . .

He even had ideas about labels. The zoo's exhibits should be identified in the same way the best museums were just beginning to identify their specimens—not only with an animal's Latin and common names, but also with something about its natural environment, and with an indication of where in the world it is found in its wild state. He had never seen zoo animals labeled to his satisfaction.

That summer the Zoological Society sent him and Mrs. Hornaday on an inspection tour of the best zoological gardens of Europe. In London, Amsterdam, Rotterdam, The Hague, Antwerp, Berlin, Hamburg, Cologne, Frankfort, and Paris he observed what to imitate, and what to avoid. He filled eight notebooks with comments and sketches.

In the fall he was back in the Bronx, making a survey of what would be his domain. Each day Mrs.

Hornaday brought along a picnic lunch. With a one-hundred-foot tape measure and a load of homemade surveyors' pins for markers they went over the glades and forests, ridges and valleys, and the bogs, lake, and river of Bronx Park. Gratefully he recalled his course in surveying and map-making at Iowa State College, twenty-five years earlier.

Then plans were drawn up. Buildings for animals—dens, aviaries, shelters, ranges, corrals. An administration building, too. And another idea occurred to him. The Society should publish a magazine, popularly written, well illustrated, about its work, about the zoo. It would be sent to all who joined the Society. It became the first such publication, setting an example that would be followed by a thousand zoos and museums across the country.

When the zoo was almost ready, he permitted some newsmen to come up to Bronx Park and look around. "FINE QUARTERS FOR ANIMALS" read the headline in the *New York Times*. The journalists loved the animal ranges, the beaver pond, the bear dens, the huge reptile house that was the largest in the world. But they were most fascinated with the flying cage, an eighty-foot-high enclosure still under construction. In it were trees and a little river, making a perfectly natural home for herons, bitterns, egrets, sea fowl, and other birds.

Opening day at the zoo finally came, on November 9, 1899, at three o'clock in the afternoon. An outdoor auditorium had been set up in front of the aquatic bird house, which was decorated with red, white, and blue bunting for the occasion. Chairs were placed around for the many invited guests of the Society. Two special trains had brought them to the park.

At a flag-draped speaker's stand, one of the zoo's founders, Professor Henry Fairfield Osborn, got up to speak. "What our museums are doing for art and natural science," he said, "this park will do for nature, by bringing its wonders and beauties within reach of thousands and millions of all classes who cannot travel and explore."

The zoo opened with 843 specimens of 157 species. Several thousand visitors were there on opening day to see them.

Since the big flying cage was still not ready for visitors, the chief attraction was the Reptile House. In it were forty snakes and a row of pools containing twenty-one species of terrapin, including a 40-pound green turtle. Palm trees and other suitably tropical plants in the building contributed to the atmosphere.

Some of the zoo's animals, unaccustomed to publicity, were shy. The big red Russian wolf scurried to a rock at the farthest corner of his cage. A little brown bear quickly climbed a tree when he saw a crowd approaching his den.

But four California sea lions kept on barking and barking, and an indulgent public chose to interpret their noise as a sign of welcome.

8
Forty Years' War for Wild Life

Hornaday thoroughly enjoyed directing the zoo. Sometimes he would complain that he spent too much of his time in a swivel chair, answering hundreds of questions, making out reports, and deciding just what diet the newly arrived Australian platypus must have to survive in New York. But he also nursed sick chimpanzees, conducted guided tours of the park for visiting dignitaries, traveled to Montana and Wyoming to inspect America's northern wild animals, went to Europe to buy lions and tigers, and did a lot more.

At times he felt like a stage manager watching his actors go through their paces. The most exciting part of the show often took place behind the scenes, after the audience had gone.

When the zoo opened, two of its most popular inhabitants were a pair of large male polar bears who lived in a den with a swimming pool. They wrestled fiercely with each other, but it was all in fun. Several years later one of them became ill and died. The survivor seemed lonely and depressed. It was suggested that a female companion be introduced, but Hornaday was afraid to take a chance with a female. The male could easily murder her; but even if he did not, Hornaday feared the rough play would soon wear her out.

The polar bear handler from whom Hornaday had purchased the two males was so sure there would be no trouble that he offered to return half the purchase price of a female if anything happened. The zoo's most experienced bear keeper also believed that there would be no trouble. So the female came to the zoo that winter.

She was placed in a temporary cage at the side of the polar bear den. The two animals seemed happy to be together, even though they were separated by two sets of bars. They licked each others' noses, and ate and slept side by side.

After three harmonious weeks Hornaday and the bear keeper decided to put the newcomer into the den. But they prepared for trouble anyway. Five keepers were on hand, with spike poles, long iron bars, lariats, wooden planks, and a large supply of meat.

Hornaday gave the order. "Open the den door, just a foot. Let her put her head out. Keep him away."

The female put her head through the narrow opening. The male stood back, so the next order was given.

"Let her go!"

She went into the den. In an instant the male was upon her. Hornaday and the keepers tried to hold him off. They beat him over the head, they pushed steel spikes into him, they rammed him with planks. As soon as they drove him away the female would try to rise; but the male would be back again the next second, throwing her down in the snow and ice, trying to reach her throat.

For twenty minutes or longer the battle raged despite all the keeper's efforts. Only when the male dragged the helpless female to a corner of the den far from the entrance could one of the keepers safely go in and throw a lasso. He noosed the bear's neck, and handed the end of the rope out through the bars to Hornaday and the other keepers. Ten hands eagerly pulled the bear back toward the bars, away from his victim. Then another rope was thrown over him in case the first should break, and two keepers were able to go in and drag the female back to safety.

But it was too late. At the last minute the big bear's teeth had torn into her jugular vein, and she died only minutes after her rescue.

Hornaday a thousand times regretted his decision. For long afterward he said that he would not, for five thousand dollars, see such a thing again. But he still could not blame the beast for outright murder. He believed that the animal only intended to play, as he had with his earlier male comrade, but that the joy of combat had seized him. "Murder in the second degree," he used to say whenever he told the story.

The personalities of the zoo's inhabitants always fascinated the director. One of his favorites was a lady

elephant who had performed at Coney Island's Luna Park. Hornaday nicknamed her "Dainty Alice," because she was anything but ladylike. She showed this only four days after she came to the zoo.

Alice was being taken out for her daily exercise when she was startled by the roar of a nearby mountain lion. Suddenly breaking away from her two keepers, she headed straight for the Reptile House. They grabbed the only part of her they could reach —her ears. One at each side of her head, they were dragged along as she went through the building full of caged snakes and out the opposite door. A crowd of the zoo's visitors screamed and ran in all directions.

A short time later the confused animal returned to the Reptile House. By this time Hornaday had arrived on the scene. As Alice went through the doorway leading into the main hall he and the two keepers grabbed her front feet and chained them to the guard rail, whose steel posts were set deep in concrete. Alice tried to pull out the posts, but they held fast. Three zoo men camped there for the night, feeding Alice hay and bread to distract her from the plate-glass cages of venomous cobras, rattlesnakes, moccasins, and bushmasters.

In the morning a fresh group of keepers arrived. They chained the elephant's front legs together so that she could only hobble a short distance at a time. Then they released her from the restraining posts and tried to turn her around to go out the way she had entered. But she would not turn and, hobbled as she was, she went right through the main hall, butting the glass cages with her powerful head and trunk. Boom!

Bang! Smash! Hornaday and his staff heard and saw the cages crash down. Fourteen small rattlesnakes were writhing through broken glass on the floor.

Finally, poking at her with their elephant hooks, they headed her out of the building. They steered her over to a stand of maple trees and, attaching each leg to a different tree, they left her on her side for twenty-four hours. Then the keepers turned their attention to the snakes, which were caught and put in new cages.

In the meantime Hornaday had telephoned her former keeper, Dick Richards, in Coney Island. Richards agreed to come to the zoo as Alice's keeper.

Several years later he would be faced with the job of moving Alice to the new Elephant House, half a mile across the park. When the time came her left leg was attached to one end of a one-hundred-foot length of the strongest rope. Richards led her a few paces at a time. Just before she reached her new home, Alice stopped and absolutely refused to move.

Twenty laborers were working on the grounds nearby. Hornaday called them. Each man found a place along the long rope. In a hilarious tug of war, they finally heaved Dainty Alice into her new apartment.

Life at the zoo was enlivened with such happy events as the long-awaited arrival of rare pygmy hippopotamuses from Africa, or the birth of new animal babies at the zoo. When coyote babies were born one spring, Hornaday made notes of their progress:

"Tame coyote Medora gave birth to litter of 4 young night of April 26. Examined on the 30th, weight 12 oz. Eyes of first opened May 12. Changed mother and young on May 11 to other den. She became quite excited and carried one around in her mouth for half an hour. We thought she had killed it, but she had not hurt it. Would not give it up to keeper. Mother took them out for the first time on May 14. Photographed May 24. Howled first time, May 25 & began to fight."

Andrew Carnegie had been a generous patron of the Zoological Society since 1896, when Hornaday had suggested him as a member of its board. Years later, on a June morning, the aging benefactor paid what was to be his last visit to the zoo. Hornaday had arranged that they would drive through the park, breaking every rule and riding right over walks and paths that were supposed to be restricted to pedestrians. He had also arranged for the keepers of the largest animals to fling food into the corrals and outdoor dens as the car came in sight. As the millionaire passed each animal enclosure, he was delighted to find the wild beasts rushing up, as it seemed, to greet him.

One of the proudest moments in Hornaday's life came when King Albert of Belgium visited the zoo. Following the invasion of his country in 1914, the king himself had led his armies into battle, and his heroic resistance had captured the imagination of the American people. Now, after the war, he, his queen, and the crown prince made a triumphal tour of the United States.

Hornaday found him a true hero, ". . . a king so kingly," he said, "that when I saw him I gladly would have filched his handkerchief as a souvenir of a royal man."

The New York Zoological Society was presenting a fine collection of birds, mammals, and reptiles to the Antwerp Zoo, the finest in Belgium, which was being rebuilt after it had been severely damaged during the war. Hornaday had the pleasure of telling the royal family about the gift.

When King Albert's visit to the zoo was over, he thanked his host and added, "I shall send you a decoration, Dr. Hornaday."

He did. It was the Cross of the Order of the Crown of Belgium. "And so," said Hornaday, "I did not need the king's handkerchief."

An aim of the New York Zoological Society, stated in its charter, was "the preservation of our native animals." It was one of the things that had attracted Hornaday to the Society. He believed that it was the first scientific organization ever to have wildlife conservation as a declared purpose.

Although his duties as director of the zoo did not require him to contribute to this part of the society's work, he volunteered to take it on. He promised that his conservation activities would not cause him to neglect his directorial tasks. He also made it clear that he expected no addition to his salary for this extra work.

It was a cause that was close to his heart, and already he had left his mark on the conservation movement in America. There was a small buffalo herd in Washington to prove it. He had written about the extermination of the American bison, but because of his efforts that event never took place.

So even while he was designing the zoo, he set to

work on this new project. He decided to make a survey, comparing the wildlife situation at that moment with what it had been fifteen years earlier. Painstakingly he located the names and addresses of about 250 knowledgeable people—ornithologists, sportsmen, hunting guides, taxidermists—two or more in each state or territory. From his one-man office letters went out: Which species were increasing? Which just holding their own? Which had decreased in fifteen years, and how much? Which were now on the verge of extinction?

The answers proved the seriousness of the situation. Virtually every state reported a severe loss in bird life. The average for thirty states was 46 per cent over fifteen years. Only four states reported an increase in their bird populations.

A man in Carnegie, Pennsylvania, wrote that "in traveling through the country I do not see more than about one-third as many birds as I did fifteen years ago." From his home state of Iowa came a report that of birds of prey, one-half remain; of water fowl, one-third; game birds, one-tenth. As the game birds disappeared, hunters were going after song and insectivorous species. A Washington, D. C., correspondent had written that 2,600 robins had been received from North Carolina in one month by a dealer who was selling them as food.

Even the buffalo were not out of danger. Only a few years earlier a group of poachers had attacked the wild bison herd in Yellowstone National Park. Three hundred animals had been reduced to thirty between 1890 and 1893. One culprit was caught literally red-handed, in the act of skinning seven of the Park's cows. But he could not be punished for his assault on national property, because there were no laws prescribing a penalty for his deed.

And the buffalo were only one species to have felt the effects of destruction. Passenger pigeons, once numbering in the billions, had been completely exterminated. In Alaska the fur seals were being depleted by poachers, who wasted three-quarters of their kill. Several states reported that bears, white-tailed deer, elk, even otters and beaver were nearly extinct. Antelope, mountain sheep, white goats, mule deer, moose, caribou—all were vanishing rapidly.

Hornaday reported these findings in "The Destruction of our Birds and Mammals," published in the Zoological Society's *Second Annual Report* in 1898.

It was the first of a long series of articles, books, pamphlets, and letters on the subject. He worked for state and national game preserves, the protection of the Alaskan fur seal, and a permanent ban on hunting any species threatened with extinction. With equal vigor he opposed the use of all automatic guns for hunting, the sale of wild game, and the killing of insect-eating birds and songbirds for food and of all birds for hat decorations.

He tirelessly addressed, through their newspapers, the people of every state where animal life was threatened, where a bill regulating hunting or the sale of game was being voted on. He wrote directly to state and national legislators. He testified more than once before congressional committees. The Congress was told in no uncertain terms that greater protection of native birds and animals was its urgent duty. He even told the President what his duty was to American wildlife.

In 1905 the Zoological Society offered to give a herd of fifteen bison to the nation if the Government would donate a suitable range and provide maintenance for the herd. The result was the 12-square mile Wichita National Bison Range, established in southwestern Oklahoma in 1908 with nine female and six male bison from the New York Zoo. Protected, they increased and survived. By 1912 this herd had grown to thirty-nine, and was the pride and joy of the Zoological Society.

As soon as the zoo's bison were in their new Oklahoma home, Hornaday decided that the project should be imitated elsewhere in the country. He founded the American Bison Society, to buy buffalo to stock other Government-created preserves. The first place to catch his eye was in Montana. If the Government would provide eighteen square miles of the Flathead Range and $40,000 for maintenance, the Society agreed to give $10,000 worth of animals.

To members of the congressional committee investigating the proposal it seemed like a good idea. But no one had ever heard of the American Bison Society. Would it live up to its share of the deal? The lawmakers were sceptical, and the bill seemed stalled in committee.

Hornaday decided to call upon an old acquaintance, President Theodore Roosevelt. They had met first in 1887, when Hornaday was working on his bison display for the National Museum.

Since that time they had enjoyed many a conversation about the wildlife of the world, and exchanged stories of their hunting adventures. One day at lunch, the zoo director had apologized to the President for taking so much of his time with what he called "shop talk."

President Roosevelt had glared. "Hornaday," he said fiercely, "if I could not—once in a while—meet a man like you and talk with him about animals, and forget other matters—I should die!"

So Hornaday went to the White House, this time on business.

"What can I do for you?" asked the President.

"Please send for the two Republican committee members, tell them that our Montana bison bill is all right, that the Bison Society is all right, and that we will do all we promise if this bill is passed."

"All right. Leave it to me."

And presently thirty-seven buffalo went to their new range near Ravalli, Montana.

Fifty years later, as a result of these beginning efforts and others that followed, there would be over 8,000 bison in the National Park system.

Meanwhile the Zoological Society drew up a model bill for New York's state legislature, stronger than any conservation law anywhere. It prohibited, forever and completely, the sale of wild native game in the state. Known as the Bayne Bill for the state senator who sponsored it, it became a law in New York. The Bayne Law became a model for other states in which the Zoological Society helped effect a conservation program.

One of the Zoological Society's biggest projects was

104

its lobbying in Congress in 1912 for the passage of a bill to protect migratory game and insectivorous birds. To provide material for this and other campaigns, Hornaday surveyed the conservation scene again. In the resulting book, *Our Vanishing Wild Life,* he listed each state and announced its failures in protecting its wildlife. Giving one example after another, he spelled out the need for protection on a national scale.

"I have been a sportsman myself," he wrote, "but times have changed, and we must change also. When game was plentiful, I believed that it was right for men and boys to kill a limited amount of it for sport and for the table." But, he added, "the three million gunners of today must no longer expect or demand the same generous hunting privileges that were right for hunters fifty years ago, when game was fifty times as plentiful as it is now, and there was only one killer for every fifty now in the field."

He wrote also of the people's rights in their natural heritage. By "game" he meant both birds and mammals. "The game of North America does not belong wholly and exclusively to the men who kill! The other ninety-seven per cent of the People have vested rights in it, far exceeding those of the three per cent. Posterity has claims upon it that no honest man can ignore."

The Zoological Society raised $11,000 to mail *Our Vanishing Wild Life* to thousands of people all over the country. More than 5,000 copies went to state legislators alone. Members of sportsmen's clubs, all of the state and territorial governors, and the justices of the

Supreme Court were others who got copies of the book. Every member of the Senate and the House of Representatives got his copy in time to read it thoroughly before voting on the bird protection bill. A few months later that bill was passed. It was a triumph for the Zoological Society and Hornaday. His work for the wild animals he loved was never ended. He retired as the zoo's director in 1926, having been there for thirty years. He found time, both before and after his retirement, to write many books about his hunting adventures and his animal friends. And he devoted most of his time to the wild-life Protection Fund, which he had established some years before. He had raised more than $100,000 for this project.

Every year on his birthday *The New York Times* sent a reporter to interview him. On December 2, 1933 the *Times* headline was "DR. HORNADAY AT 79 RECALLS THE BISON. WILD LIFE CONSERVATIONIST LOOKS BACK WITH SATISFACTION OVER 55-YEAR FIGHT."

And the nation's leading elder statesman of zoology said to the reporter: "I have seen the American bison saved from total extinction; I have seen the fur seal industry in Alaska saved; I have seen the passage of many good laws, both State and Federal.

"But I have seen the guns increase faster than the game protectors. We have not yet caught up with the front line of the guns."

There was still work for him to do.

William Temple Hornaday died on March 6, 1937. His health had been poor for about a year.

In its obituary *The New York Times* reported, "One of Mr. Hornaday's last acts was to write to President Franklin D. Roosevelt a week ago, asking the President to use his influence to save the remnant of wild life in the United States. He received a reply from the President expressing sympathy because of his illness and assuring him that he would do everything possible to carry out his request."

At his funeral, "Home on the Range" and "Trees" were sung. At his grave, "Taps" was sounded by Boy Scout buglers.

One July morning years after his death—it was in 1957—workmen were taking down an old exhibit of bison in the National Museum's Natural History Building. In the plaster earth underneath a large buffalo they uncovered a rusty metal box.

In it were two issues of *Cosmopolitan* magazine from 1887. They contained a two-part article by William T. Hornaday, "The Passing of the Buffalo."

At the top of one article was a note:

"To my Illustrious Successor:

"Dear Sir:

Enclosed please find a brief and truthful account of the capture of the specimens which compose this group. The old bull, the young cow and the yearling calf were killed by yours truly.

"When I am dust and ashes I beg you to protect these specimens from deterioration and destruction. Of course they are crude productions in comparison with what you produce, but you must remember

107

that at this time (A.D. 1888, March 7) the
American School of Taxidermy has only just been
recognized. Therefore give the devil his due, and
revile not

W. T. Hornaday.''

The bison, seventy years after Hornaday put them there, were slightly faded but otherwise in good condition. He would have been pleased. And his wish was heeded. The Smithsonian will continue to display them.

Nature Projects You Can Do

Animal life is all around you, waiting to be discovered by you.

This may seem impossible—you live in a tall apartment house in the middle of a large city, or in a community where every lawn is hedged to keep unwanted creatures out. But it is true. Probably not one hour from where you are sitting right now is a place where the patient, quiet observer can discover signs of animal life.

Not everyone will find every animal mentioned in this section. (Some lucky readers will be able to find other, even more interesting examples.) And not everyone will want or be able to do all of the suggested projects. But everyone can find *some* animal activity, suited to his interests and circumstances, in the paragraphs that follow.

1. Your Nature Notebook

You are now a junior zoologist, planning a field trip. Your nature notebook is your most basic project. No scientist investigates anything without making careful records. Date, weather, time of day, where you went, what you were looking for, what you found—all go into your journal. You may later use your notes as the basis for labels in a home nature museum, to remind you of something when you write a report for school, to help you identify an animal or its tracks, or just to recall a pleasant day spent in getting close to nature. A pocketsize spiral or looseleaf notebook will be best, and don't forget the pens or pencils.

Perhaps you are interested in sketching or drawing animals. Take along a small sketch pad—about 5 by 9 inches—and drawing pencils. Your school or public library probably has books on drawing animals which will give your some pointers. When you get home you may want to use your sketches as the basis of clay models. (Hornaday taught himself, at an early stage in his career, to sketch and draw. He carried pads, pencils, and paints with him on his field trips, and kept his own graphic records of the shape, movement, and natural coloring of every animal he observed. This was in the days before photography became popular. He also taught himself to model in clay.)

2. *Looking for Signs of Animal Life*

To track or trail an animal is an adventure for the beginner as well as the experienced hunter or zoologist. Although there may be more opportunities for those who live in the country or the suburbs, even the city dweller can find the place and the time to get on the animal trail.

Where to look: Open fields, meadows, pastures, along a road, near a pond, hillsides, along the banks of streams, in the woods—the possibilities are endless. In the city, explore the parks, riverbanks, or lake shores. Even cemeteries and city dumps are places to look. Study a map of your city and the surrounding area; you'll surely discover several likely places for animal exploration. A train or car ride of an hour or less is very likely to land the city dweller near a state park or game preserve; or a day or weekend trip to a national park might

be planned. Perhaps the whole family might get interested in making some of these nature projects the focus of a summer vacation.

When to look. Few animals are up and about during the day. Most prefer the in-between hours near dawn or dusk for their food-gathering; and some animals are about only at night. A cloudy day might fool some creatures into staying active. Otherwise the very early morning or late afternoon are the best times for viewing animals in nature. Summer or winter, most animals have to get food, and so they can be seen at any season. Most animals, however, are likely to be elusive and remain hidden. But you can become a good animal detective and find evidence of their presence, even when they themselves cannot be seen. And the daylight hours are fine for this. Animal tracks can be found at any season of the year.

What to look for. Animal homes, tracks, marks on trees

can all be seen; animal calls can be heard. Look for tracks in clay-type soil, in snow or mud, on sandy beaches, in the woods after a rain, or near a stream. Look for trampled-on foliage in a narrow path that indicates a trail. Look for bits of fur or feathers, telling perhaps the story of a fight. You might find a small carcass as conclusive evidence of an animal battle; or a battered little furry body along a road, evidence of man's unwanted intrusion. Look for the remains of an animal's meal: nutshells, gnawed pine cones, and the like. Look for animal marks on trees: branches cut off by beavers or woodchucks, worn spots where a deer rubbed the fuzz off his new antlers, claw or tooth marks.

How to look. Silence is the first essential. If an animal hears you, you will never get a chance to see it. Animals can also smell you, so if you think there is something there make sure you are standing in a place where the wind is blowing from the animal's direction to you, and not the other way around. If necessary, move around in a semi-circle so your scent is not carried.

If you locate a good spot where there is animal activity— near an animal's home, a watering place, or feeding grounds

—you might want to build a *blind* to conceal yourself while you wait patiently and watch whatever goes on. A blind is merely a sort of camouflaged tent, with peepholes. Perhaps the simplest is the umbrella blind, made by inserting an old beach umbrella into the ground. Paint the fabric dark green or brown, and attach a "curtain" of dark fabric all round it (a large old bedsheet can be dyed and dropped right over the umbrella spike). Pegs of wood can be hammered through the fabric into the ground in several places to keep the tent from flapping in the breeze. Cut a slit in the tent at a comfortable height for you to look out, and your blind is ready. Another simple type of blind can be made by constructing a lean-to of poles and draping fabric over it in similar fashion.

Perhaps you would like to try *baiting* to attract animals. If you know what animals are in the vicinity, find out what food they like and provide some. Rock salt, fresh meat, nuts, cereal, or bread crumbs are some possibilities.

3. Hunting with a Camera

A camera is a good companion along the trail. You can photograph tracks, homes, or the animal itself. The day after a snowstorm is often an ideal time to find animal tracks clear enough to show up in photographs. This is a good way to learn about an animal's adventures during the preceeding night. Perhaps the tracks will tell the story of a cottontail rabbit moving about slowly at first, in changing directions, as he feeds; then the tracks suddenly dart off in a straight line indicating that a fox has come up behind him. The trail ends at a hole in a stone wall, and you can guess that the rabbit has escaped. Or perhaps, where the trail stops, there is no stone wall, but the snow is flattened from the wing tips of a great horned owl which, you imagine, must have swooped down from the sky. Perhaps bits of fur and a few feathers in the snow tell the rest of a story that ends tragically. All of this could be photographed and then written up in your nature notebook.

Mammals may be hard to find in the daytime, but birds are good subjects for the camera fan. A bird feeder placed close to a window in winter will attract many winged creatures. Such birds as the downy woodpecker, chickadee, and white-breasted nuthatch are attracted to suet, while the cardinal, blackbird, mourning dove and numerous varieties of sparrows will come to eat grain or wild bird seed.

If you have found a fresh bird's nest you can be almost certain that the bird will soon show up to pose for your camera. You might want to construct a blind near the nest, or near your feeding station, so that you can remain hidden while you take your pictures. The umbrella blind, described previously, is suitable for this. Be careful to put it up in such a way that you will not be aiming the camera into the sun. About four feet from the nest or feeder is a good distance for a photographic blind, but you should first set it up about 20 feet away to give the birds a chance to get used to it. Move it several times, a few feet at a time, until it is in position.

Nighttime animal photography. Animals such as the fox, raccoon, skunk, or possum are active only at night, and they are so wary that it would be almost impossible to locate and get close enough to them to get good photographs. However, you can trick them into taking their own pictures by setting a camera trap in an area where you know they are likely to be. Perhaps you can accustom them to coming to the area by leaving food for them every evening.

Equipment for a *camera trap:* camera with shutter release lever and attached synchronized flash gun (use an inexpensive box-type camera, as it will be left outdoors); spool of strong black thread; a snap mousetrap; a wooden peg or small pole; a screw eye; heavy-duty twine or adhesive tape; a plastic food-wrap bag; and some food (beef bones, vegetables, fruit) to bait the camera trap.

Using twine or adhesive tape, fasten camera and flash equipment to a tree at a downward angle, focussing it on the place where you will leave the food. If necessary, use a piece of wood as a wedge to tilt the camera to the proper position.

114

Fasten the mousetrap to the tree with its spring bar in a downward position. Hammer the peg into the ground and twist the screw eye into the top of the peg. Attach one end of a long piece of black thread to the bait. Run the other end through the screw eye. Pull it up tight and tie it to the bait hook of the mousetrap. Attach a second, shorter piece of string loosely to the bar spring of the mousetrap and the other end to the shutter release of the camera. Cover the camera and flash attachment with the plastic bag, cutting out a hole in front of the lens and making sure the bag clears the shutter.

Now (be careful not to catch your fingers!) set the mousetrap and test the equipment by pulling the bait to make sure it works smoothly. Load the camera with film; place a bulb in the flash attachment. If other people are likely to come that way, it might be a good idea to leave a note explaining that you have set a camera trap and asking them not to disturb it. When the animal comes to get the food, it will pull the thread which springs the mousetrap which, in turn, pulls the shutter release—and the animal thus takes its own picture.

4. Collecting Casts of Tracks.

This makes an unusual collection and is not difficult to do.

Equipment: soft brush, plaster of paris, a small bowl or can (a plastic refrigerator dish is good) for mixing the plaster, a spoon or stick, a strip of cardboard or strong oak tag 1 inch wide, water, and a paper clip.

First select the clearest footprint you can find. Using the brush, remove twigs, leaves, small stones, and excess dirt from inside the track or around it. Take the strip of cardboard and place it in a circle about 1 or 2 inches around the track. Overlap the ends of the cardboard and fasten with the paper clip. Push the cardboard ring carefully into the dirt to form a dam for your plaster. Pour some water into the can or bowl (about a third of the amount of plaster that you think you will need). Pour in plaster until it rises above the surface of the water. Then stir with spoon or stick until mixture is smooth. It should have the consistency of thick cream. When it is ready, pour it slowly over the track. It should come halfway up the side of the cardboard. Allow 30 minutes for the plaster to set, and remove the cardboard collar. While the plaster is still soft you can put a staple or hook on the back or top so it can be easily hung on the wall. When set, remove collar and lift out cast. Brush to clean. You can later paint the track one color and the rest of the plaster a second color, or you may prefer to leave the track white and paint the surrounding part of the plaque. A coat of shellac will protect your casting. Your collection of track castings can include those of birds as well as mammals—many different kinds of wildlife can decorate your walls.

5. Live-catch Traps for Small Animals

Mice, rats, shrews, and other small animals can be captured alive in specially designed traps. Live-catch traps can be purchased commercially, or you can easily make your own.

To make a trap for small animals you will need: an ordinary mousetrap, a No. 2 can, a 6-inch-square piece of 1/4-inch wire mesh, metal-cutting shears, wire or strong adhesive tape.

Using metal shears, cut into one side of the can near the top to make a rectangular opening that just fits the trigger of the mousetrap. Place the can in position on the trap, with the trigger in the opening, and fasten the can to the base of the trap with wire or adhesive tape. Cut the wire mesh into a square a little larger than the can opening. Wire the edges of the mesh square to the square loop of the mousetrap. Set the trap, using appropriate bait (bread crumbs, crushed bacon, salted nuts, peanut butter, sunflower seeds and ham rind). When the trap is sprung, the wire mesh will form a lid for

the can, permitting the trapped animals to breathe until you release him into his cage. (This is known as the Hatt trap, for the man who designed it.)

Place traps where animals are likely to come: near nests, alongside fallen trees, where you have previously discovered evidence of an animal's meal. Scatter some bait near the trap as well as in it.

When you come to collect your animals, bring along a small laundry bag or flour sack (clean, of course). Hold the sack over the trap; open the trap while it is inside the sack and shake the animal out. Then you can move it from the sack to its cage.

6. Your Small Animal Zoo.

The first step in planning a collection of live animals is to get permission—from your parents if you intend to start a zoo in your home, or from school authorities if a science class or club undertakes this project. In some states it will also be necessary to get permission from the state game department to keep wild animals, even small ones, captive.

Next, decide what animals to keep, and learn what the proper cages, proper food, and proper care are for each variety. Very young squirrels, raccoons, skunks, and 'possums are usually preferred, because they have not gotten used to life in the wild: they will adapt more readily to cages and frequent handling than will older ones. Native mice and rats, turtles, snakes, and the other animals discussed below are some additional possibilities. Many of these can be purchased at pet stores. Some can be caught alive, in commercial traps or in ones you have made yourself (see project 5, above).

Cages should be large enough for the animals to get some exercise; should be easy to clean; and should be convenient for feeding the occupants. Cages of various sizes and designs can be purchased at pet stores, or you can make your own.

To make your own small animal cage you will need: metal shears, $\frac{1}{4}$-inch wire mesh in a suitable size (a cage 8 by 9 by 6 inches will require a piece of wire mesh 20 by 21 inches; a cage 12 by 18 by 10 inches will require a piece of wire mesh 32 by 38 inches), a board of the length and width of the finished cage, strong metal staples or tacks.

Using metal shears, cut the wire mesh as indicated in the diagram (dimensions are given for the 8-by-9-by-6-inch cage). Cut a square piece out of one side larger than your hand, as shown. Cut another piece of mesh for the door, slightly larger than this door opening.

Bend the rough edges of the door opening and the door down with pliers, or cover with a narrow strip of adhesive cloth tape. Loosely wire the door into place over the door opening, so that it moves freely as on a hinge. A small "loop buttonhole" of wire at the bottom of the door can fit over a small wire "button" to close the door firmly.

Bend the wire mesh as indicated by the dotted lines in diagram A. Wire adjoining 6-inch edges together. Place cage in position over board, and staple or tack it firmly to the sides of the board. See diagram B.

Some possible pets for your zoo:
Guinea pigs make excellent pets and are easy to raise. The best covering materials for their cage floor are litter, sawdust, or fine wood chips. To keep them clean and odorless, the cage covering should be changed every other day and never allowed to remain more than 2 days. Hay is good to keep as a material for these animals to sleep in, and they will also eat

120

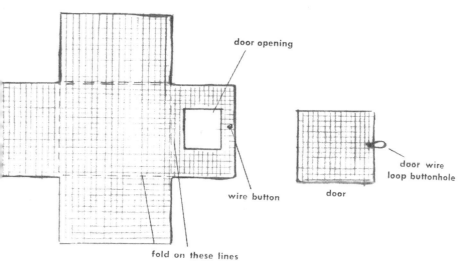

door opening

door wire
loop buttonhole

wire button   door

fold on these lines

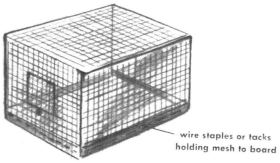

wire staples or tacks
holding mesh to board

it. Their food may be regular guinea-pig food (from any pet
store), rabbit pellets, grain, fresh vegetables (other than
lettuce), or kibbled dog food. Fresh water should always be
in the cage.

Domestic rats are among the best pets for an indoor zoo.
They are better to keep than mice as they lack the strong odor
of mice and are less quarrelsome. White and hooded rats are
two of the better known varieties. Unless rats are handled regu-
larly, they may bite. Floor covering for rats should be sawdust or fine wood chips. Hay and bits of cloth or paper make

121

good bedding for their nest box. For food, grain (especially oats), flax and hemp, or special dog mix with green vegetables are satisfactory. When there are babies, both the mother and her litter should have bread and milk. A small, fat bone, free of grease, is fine for bone-building food as well as for fun. *Domestic rabbits* for an indoor zoo should be limited to the smaller varieties. Rabbits are basically out-of-doors creatures, and need spacious cages and plenty of fresh air and room to run about. Cover their cage floor with sawdust, fine wood chips, or litter. Floor covering should be changed every two days. Food consists of rabbit pellets, purchased from any pet store, hay, oats, and greens, as well as carrots, beets and lettuce. Fresh water should be in the cage at all times. *Snakes* are usually easy to keep. A snake cage should be of glass (wire often hurts the snakes mouths when they rub against it), with a wire-mesh lid to allow ventilation. A large glass aquarium fitted with a wire-mesh cover set in a wooden frame is a good cage. The cage should be as long as the snake, and half as wide and half as high as it is long. Most small snakes will be well taken care of in a box about 12 by 6 by 6 inches. Two or three small snakes can be kept in such a cage at once. The floor may be left plain, or some rounded pebbles or sand may be added. The floor can also be covered with newspaper to simplify cleaning. Most snakes should have a branch or shelf to drape themselves from. Water should be kept in the cage at all times, preferably in a low dish in the center of the floor. Cages must be cleaned often and all excreta removed as snakes become infected and get diseased when cages are not clean and there is too much moisture.

Snakes can endure long periods of not eating. Small snakes feed about once a week, while larger ones can go several weeks without food. All snakes eat less often in winter—about once a month. Most snakes feed on live food, so keep chopped fresh meat or fish, plus a supply of insects and earthworms. Those snakes that are difficult to feed can be exhibited in your indoor zoo for several weeks and then liberated and others collected in their place. As snakes are cold-blooded animals they must always be kept suitably warm if they are to remain active and healthy—the temperature should not fall below 65°F.

To collect snakes, search along old fences, stone walls, in brush piles, and under logs. Most harmless kinds can easily be taken in your hands; few bite, and if they do it is only a minor scratch. Larger varieties can be collected with the aid of a forked stick or tweezers placed just behind the head. You are most likely to find garter snakes, ribbon snakes, green or grass snakes, DeKay brown snakes, ring-necked snakes, and hog-nosed snakes. Among the larger varieties are the black snake in the East, and the bull snake, chicken snake, king snake, and the very large indigo snake in the southern, central, and western parts of the country.

Turtles, both water-dwelling and those that live on the land, are good indoor zoo exhibits. For the water turtles you can get large shallow plastic pans from a hardware store, or you can use glass aquariums. One end of your container should have water deep enough so the turtles can swim, but the other end should have rocks or a board on which they can climb out whenever they wish to rest or enjoy a sunbath. Feed them raw chopped meat or earthworms and insects. Change the water after feeding as meat left in water any length of time will foul the water and give out a strong odor. Turtles should be fed every other day, or not less than 3 times a week. You can probably find the painted turtle, spotted turtle, musk or mud turtle, and small snapping turtle near ponds and capture them for your indoor zoo. You can purchase yellow-bellied terrapin at most pet stores.

Land turtles can be kept in an open wire cage with a metal bottom or in an aquarium. The bottom should have soil, sand, if possible a potted plant, some small rocks, and a shallow pan of water. The box turtle and wood turtle are easily collected from damp woods and swamps. Feed them earthworms, sliced carrots, lettuce, fresh raw meat, and insects. Water should be changed after each feeding and sand and soil cleaned or changed every 2 weeks.

123

Small snakes, toads, tree frogs, spring peepers, or wood frogs can be kept in a *woodland terrarium*. You can make one out of a glass aquarium by covering the bottom with coarse gravel and adding soil and leaf mold to a depth of about 2 inches. Plant ferns, mosses, small flowering plants, club moss, and little seedlings of white pine or hemlock in the soil. Add some flat rocks covered with moss or lichen to make your terrarium look very natural. Feed your terrarium animals earthworms, mealworms, houseflies, grasshoppers, and insects of all kinds. Spray water frequently over the terrarium, using a laundry sprinkler or house-plant atomizer, or just sprinkle by hand. Keep terrarium covered to prevent evaporation of moisture.

Keep salamanders, spotted salamanders, red salamanders, snails, tadpoles and various frogs such as the leopard frog, green frog, and bull frog in a *semi-aquatic terrarium*. Put rocks and coarse gravel at one end of a glass aquarium, and cover this with good sand and topsoil to about 2 inches. Build up the sand and topsoil in part of the aquarium to form an island, and plant the same type of plants as in the woodland terrarium. You may add ferns like the maidenhair spleenwort and a few other plants that enjoy water. When your island is finished pour in water gently (pour it over your hand so as not to disturb your planting) almost up to the level of your island. For feeding the wild life in the semi-aquatic terrarium, use insects, small fish, mealworms, earthworms, and raw meat.

7. Your Own Backyard

Early one morning, station yourself in your backyard with your nature notebook in hand, and wait and watch patiently. What do you see? Perhaps a mole's underground path, being extended, until the unseen digger finally makes a hole and comes out of his tunnel. Perhaps 2 or 3 rabbits chasing across your lawn, scouting for some goodies from your vegetable garden. Perhaps a few squirrels shaking the apples from your trees. Perhaps even a fox, scurrying by after a night's scaveng-

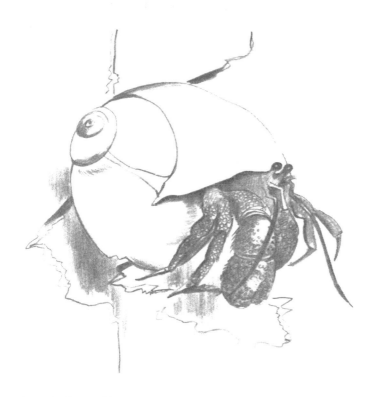

ing. And very likely a lot more. Jot it all down. And post yourself in your backyard again, at the same time and at other times, at the same season and at other seasons. Your backyard may be more exciting than you think. (The city dweller may "borrow" a backyard from a country or suburban friend or relative, or he can make a corner of a local park or vacant lot his "backyard"; it may take more patience, but some signs of wild life are bound to appear, even in a city park.)

You can be a "backyard explorer" almost anywhere—along a lake shore, near a pond, at the seashore, and so forth. The possibilities are limitless. Here is a list of 100 forms of animal life for the backyard explorer to look for. What you will find will, of course, depend upon where you live and where you are looking. See if you can locate 65 of them.

Paul G. Howes' book, *Handbook for the Curious* (G.P. Putnam) which may be found in most libraries, gives a fine sketch of most of the animals on our list. Others may be found in *Handbook of Nature Study* by Anna B. Comstock (Cornell University Press), or *Complete Field Guide for American Wild Life* by Henry Hill Collins, Jr. (Harper).

1. Boring Sponge
2. Dead Man's Fingers
3. Sea Blubber or Jellyfish
4. Sand Worm.
5. Turtle Leech
6. Earthworm
7. Starfish
8. Sand Dollar
9. Ship Barnacle
10. Sand Shrimp
11. Beach Flea
12. Crayfish
13. Sow Bug
14. Hermit Crab
15. Fiddler Crab
16. Horseshoe Crab
17. Centipede
18. Common Millipede
19. Garden Spider
20. Orb Weaving Spider
21. Grass Spider
22. Daddy Longlegs
23. Field Slug
24. Garden Snail
25. Fresh Water Mussel
26. American Oyster
27. Clam
28. Razor Clam
29. Jingle Shell
30. Oyster Drill
31. Chitan
32. Limpet
33. Periwinkle

34. Sand Collar Snail
35. Mud Snail
36. Shipworm
37. Common Skate
38. Common eel
39. Sea Herring
40. Smelt
41. Killifish
42. Sunfish
43. Horned Pout
44. Black Bass
45. Eastern Pickerel
46. Yellow Perch
47. Spotted Salamander
48. Red Backed Salamander
49. Two lined Salamander
50. Water Newt
51. American Toad
52. Spring Peeper
53. Leopard Frog
54. Green Frog
55. Bull Frog
56. Wood Frog
57. Snapping Turtle
58. Painted Terrapin
59. Spotted Turtle
60. Wood Turtle
61. Box Turtle
62. Ribbon Snake
63. Common Garter Snake
64. Common Water Snake
65. Black Snake
66. Green Snake

67. Dekays Brown Snake
68. Milk Snake
69. Hog-nosed Snake
70. Gray Squirrel
71. Chipmunk
72. Common Skunk
73. Opossum
74. Raccoon
75. White-footed Mouse
76. Ground Mole
77. Little Brown Bat
78. Short-tailed Shrew
79. Virginia Deer
80. English Sparrow
81. Starling
82. Blue Jay
83. Robin
84. Goldfinch
85. Bluebird
86. White-breasted Nuthatch
87. Chickadee
88. Downy Woodpecker
89. Song Sparrow
90. Mockingbird
91. Cat Bird
92. Cardinal
93. Chimney Swift
94. Barn Swallow
95. Hummingbird
96. Red-winged Blackbird
97. Baltimore Oriole
98. Crow
99. Herring Gull
100. Mallard Duck

8. Know your State's Conservation Program

What animals are native to your locality? What animals once native to your locality have been forced out? Have any species been reintroduced after being nearly exterminated?

What is your state doing to protect its wild life? What species are protected? How? What are the hunting rules and regulations? Where has your state established wild-life preserves? What animals are protected there? How many of each species?

Find out by writing to your state game and conservation department, at your state capital.